Gardening Tips For All Seasons – 4 In 1Bundle:

The Food Growers Top Jobs For The Autumn, Winter, Spring And Summer Planting Seasons

BY

JAMES PARIS

Blog: www.planterspost.com

Published By

www.deanburnpublications.com

ISBN-13: 978-1539380658
ISBN-10: 1539380653

Table of Contents

Episode 1: Gardening Tips For Autumn: Page 7-86

Episode 2: Gardening Tips For Winter: Page 87-132

Episode 3: Gardening Tips For Spring: Page 133-182

Episode 4: Gardening Tips For Summer: Page 183-211

**

Subjects Covered Include: seasonal gardening, vegetable growing tips, pruning fruit bushes, organic feeding, organic tea, composting, plant support, insect control, organic pesticides, raised bed gardening, small garden ideas, growing cucumber, growing tomatoes, plant care, plant support, winter vegetables.

Copyright Notice

Copyright © 2016, James Paris

All rights reserved. Copyright protected. Duplicating, reprinting or distributing this material in any form, without the express written consent of the author is prohibited.

While reasonable attempts have been made to assure the accuracy of the information contained within this publication, the author does not assume any responsibility for errors, omissions or contrary interpretation of this information, and any damages incurred by that.

The diagrams and instructions included in this book are for general guidance only; the author does not assume any responsibility or liability whatsoever, for what you choose to do with this information.

Books Included In This Bundle: 'Seasonal Gardening Jobs'

Episode 1: Gardening Tips For Autumn

Episode 2: Gardening Tips For Winter

Episode 3: Gardening Tips For Spring

Episode 4: Garden Tips For Summer

Other Relevant Books By James Paris

Raised Bed Gardening 5 Book Bundle

Companion Planting

Growing Berries

Square Foot Gardening

Compost 101

Vegetable Gardening Basics

Small Garden Ideas

Straw Bale Gardening

Hot Bed Gardening

Episode 1: Gardening Tips For Autumn:

THE FOOD GROWERS TOP 5 JOBS FOR THE FALL

Including Tasty Jam & Pickle Recipes!

BY

JAMES PARIS

BLOG: WWW.PLANTERSPOST.COM
Published By
www.deanburnpublications.com

Introduction:

Good preparation is something that everyone must pay attention to, whether it be with regards to the garden or the family or indeed every aspect of life.

The old adage that says "Failing to Prepare = preparing to fail" is so true on so many levels that I just have to include it here at the very beginning!

With regard to gardening. Whether you are into growing fruit & vegetables, flower gardening or indeed looking after acres of parkland; preparation is the key to success.

Forward planning goes a long way to ensure that you are not taken by surprise, or 'wrong footed' by some turn of events. It means that you have prepared for every eventuality (within reason), and you have 'done your homework' to ensure the best chance of success.

This is no more true than in the area of gardening where every season has its individual qualities, and the plants that grow and produce throughout these seasons have their individual needs.

Looking ahead to the next season or indeed several seasons ahead, should be the 'obsession' of every gardener, as without this valuable preparation many tasks would become unmanageable and many plants lost in a confusion of disarray.

Seasonal Issues?

With all that said, there is something else to consider with regard to seasonal garden preparation, and that is the issue of the seasons themselves.

This book for instance covers the Autumn or Fall season – the first of 4 books in this series. However in some countries or States, growing seasons are not so pronounced as to form or dictate 4 distinct time/climate zones.

The four distinctive growing seasons of Autumn, Winter, Spring and Summer that you have in Wisconsin or Minnesota for instance, are a far cry from the Florida region that has just two distinct seasons – the wet season and the dry season.

With the summer wet season lasting from May to October and the winter dry season from November through April. Neither season can be regarded as 'cold' with the lowest average winter temperature being around 40F.

Local knowledge in this respect must be down to the reader, however plans and preparations required for any successful gardener remain fundamentally the same.

Each plant will only grow and produce for a set amount of time, and forward planning is essential to keep the momentum going and for the garden to remain productive (as much as is possible) all year round.

Your time is precious, and wasted time due to poor planning, is not only time that you cannot get back – but is also bound to reflect on your gardening efforts or indeed productivity.

Outline Of Tasks Covered

Listed below is a brief outline of the gardening tasks that are highlighted in this Autumn episode.

1 - Gathering & Storing:

One of the great joys of the Fall is the aspect of bringing in the last of the fruit and vegetables, before they 'fall' to the ground or are ruined by the first frosts of winter.

In this section you will discover not only the best way to harvest your precious produce, but also how to store it over the winter period successfully.

Jam-making, pickling and other ways to preserve fruit and vegetables.

2 - Pruning:

Get your berry bushes and fruit trees put into order before the spring season, to ensure healthy survival over the winter and a bumper growth in the springtime.

Details on how to best prune your fruit bushes as well as how to take cuttings and store them for the next growing season.

3 - Continuity Planting:

Planning to grow a late Autumn crop? Check out this section to see what you can grow in cooler temperatures, or indeed what you can best grow on order to prepare the way for the main crops in spring.

Depending on where you are operating from, Autumn need not be the end of the growing season for you!

4 – Composting:

This is the time to make sure your composting efforts are at their maximum. The fall means plenty of leaf moult as well as cuttings, garden waste products etc to add to the compost heap.

Perhaps you need to consider green composting, or lasagne composting techniques to get your soil 'up to speed' for the next season?

Details of these and other techniques in this composting section.

5 – Repair & Maintenance Tasks:

Autumn is the ideal time to get your garden and various buildings, ponds, tools and all the paraphernalia associated with gardening, cleaned and sorted for winter.

1: Gathering & Storing

Most people regard the summer as the boom season when it comes to enjoying the fruits of your labour, and to a certain extent that is certainly true.

However the Fall season is also an exciting time for fruit growers especially, as the fruit tree branches sag under the weight of apples, pears, plums etc that are simply too many to be consumed in one sitting so to speak.

Fortunately there are many ways to deal with an abundant harvest of fruits, even soft fruits such as raspberries and blackberries, redcurrants and strawberries that will not store well if left on the shelf!

Most if not all fruits can be preserved by making them into jams or jellies – especially in the case of soft fruits and berries.

They can also be stored for long periods by freezing, raspberries in particular retaining strong flavours, although they do loose a little in the way of firmness.

Strictly speaking however, most of the berries and current bushes should be finished by the Fall so that the crop or harvest by this time is likely to be minimal at best.

Fruit trees even though they can be harvested throughout the summer season depending on the variety, are often laden at this time of year. And so it is with this category of fruits that I shall begin..

Harvesting & Storing Fruit:

Apples:

Apples are ready to pick when they come away easily with a little twist of the hand, with little or no resistance. Place your cupped hand under the apple and twist to remove. If the apple remains steadfast then it is not ready to harvest.

Clean the apples with a soft cloth before wrapping them individually in newspaper, and storing in a cool dry frost-free place. Any bruised fruit should not be stored, but eaten immediately or baked into a pie!

Check before storing for any insect damage, bruising, or fungal disease. Any one of these imperfections have the potential to ruin your whole harvest if stored alongside healthy fruits.

Do not store your apples near potatoes or other fruits as the ethylene gas that apples produce, will encourage ripening or in the case of potatoes, may encourage them to sprout prematurely.

Apples stored in this way can be expected to last for many weeks or even months.

<u>MY NOTES/THINGS TO DO</u>

Apricots:

Apricots are best picked <u>after</u> they have ripened on the tree, usually over a period of around three weeks or so. This means that extra care has to be taken to avoid bruising of the fruit, which should be changed from green to orange in color.

They should not be stored near other fruit such as apples especially, which let off ethylene and will encourage over-ripening.

They will store in this form for around 3 weeks if kept in a cool dry environment, however they can be dried and kept for several months.

To dry apricots, cut the fruit in half and remove the pit (seed). Leave the skins on and Press the apricot from the outside so that it is inside-out.

Place in a dehydrator for approximately 12 hours at 135F. After leaving the dried apricots on a rack to cool down, inspect to make sure they have fried out thoroughly. Seal the dried fruit in glass canning jars.

Pears:

Picking pears differs from apple picking in that pears are mostly picked <u>before</u> they ripen. If they are left to ripen on the tree they will soon succumb to insect and bird predation, they would also not last long in storage.

The pear should be picked by holding firmly in one hand and giving a gentle twist to pull the pear from the branch. Pears bruise easily even though they feel quite firm, so take care with this process.

Store in a cool dry place, where thy will last for several weeks. To store for longer periods then refrigeration is most probably needed to bring the temperature to 32&deg F to 40° F.

<u>MY NOTES/THINGS TO DO</u>

Plums:

Plums are usually harvested just as the fruit is becoming soft, and is easily pulled from the tree. However a lot depends on the variety of plum that you are growing, and sometimes it is a question of watching for a color change in the fruit as it nears maturity.

Varieties such as 'Stanley' and 'Mount Royal' for instance, change from green to dark-blue or purple before they are truly ripe.

Some other varieties have to be picked before they are truly ripe, and left for a few days in a cool dry place for the ripening process to complete.

Plums in general will not last longer than a few days or weeks after picking, depending on the variety. However they can be stored for months if dried and transformed into prunes.

To make prunes you can leave the plums until they fall (or are ready to fall) from the tree, then collect and lay them out in the sun to dry.

The downside to this method is that you will have to share your plums with the local wildlife – wasps especially have a fondness for ripe plums!

Alternatively you can wash the plums and dry with paper towels. Cut and remove the stones before placing them in a dehydrator; or oven set to around 140F for about 10-12 hours (less for a fan-assisted oven).

As a general rule, it is best to 'cook' on a lower temperature for a longer period rather than try to rush the process.

Prunes can be frozen or stored for many months in an air-tight container.

Peaches:

Peaches are harvested when they are fully ripe on the tree. This means that extra care has to be taken to ensure the fruit is not bruised when harvesting.

They should come free with just a slight twist, then be stored in a cool place where they can last for up to ten days.

Peaches can be canned, frozen or turned into jam. They can also be dried by first blanching and removing the stones and skin. Cut the flesh into slices and dry in a dehydrator at 135F for 24-30 hours depending on the thickness of the slices.

Place the cool dried fruit in open jars, shaking occasionally for about one week to dry completely. Check that they are completely dry by breaking in half, they should be crisp and snap easily, before placing in an air-tight container.

If the glass container show signs of water condensing on the inside, it tells you that the peaches are not yet properly dried out.

In this case, remove and place on racks or paper to dry properly before re-instating them to the jars.

Oranges, Lemons, & Limes:

Citrus fruits in general tend to do better when left on the tree to ripen, unless frost damage is an issue. Indeed lemons and limes will only fully harvest on the branch and if picked prematurely, they will not ripen at all.

To harvest these fruits you must be careful to leave a 'plug' in the fruit when you pull it from the branch. This will prevent fungal infection of the fruit and lengthen the storage time.

You can do this not by twisting the fruit – as in the case with apples and pears for instance – but rather by turning the fruit at a right angle and pulling it away from the branch.

This will leave the end of the holding branch in the fruit and plug the gap. Alternatively, snip the fruit away from the tree with a sharp knife or clippers so that the short stem remains to plug the fruit.

Pick the fruit when it is 'full' and heavy, slightly spongy but firm to the grasp. Best test is simply to pull one from the tree and taste it for flavour and sharpness.

Limes and lemons in particular can be left on the tree for 2-3 weeks after they mature, but do not leave until they wither and dry out.

Ripe fruits will store in a cool or refrigerated place for 3 weeks or so. A popular way to preserve citrus fruits is by juicing, or by making them into jams, jellies and marmalades.

MY NOTES/THINGS TO DO

Harvesting & Storing Vegetables:

By the time that Fall comes around, many vegetables have not only been harvested already, but they have indeed been either consumed or made into pickles, frozen or otherwise preserved for consumption over the cold winter months.

This is certainly the case for tomatoes, cucumber, zucchini and other soft vegetables (ok, so tomatoes are actually a fruit I know!).

However there are a few vegetables that actually do best harvested in the colder weather of late Autumn, and these include most of the root vegetables such as carrots, parsnips, beetroot and swedes.

Other crops such as broccoli, cauliflower, brussels sprouts and winter cabbage should be ready to harvest before Christmas, and stored for the festive season in particular (is there any other time where kids will eat brussels sprouts!).

Onions at this time should be pulled up and laid on the ground to dry, before hanging up in the garden shed or other cool, frost-free environment.

Listed below are some of the most common vegetables that are harvested/stored during the Fall season.

Brussels Sprouts:

These are best harvested after a light frost, and this is done by starting at the base of the stem and snapping away the small sprouts.

The sprouts lower on the stem will mature first, and a few days later be followed by those higher up. Generally the sprouts will be ready to harvest about 80 days after planting, and are best harvested during cold weather.

Sprouts can last for 2-3 weeks if kept in the refrigerator, preferably in a container lined with kitchen towel to prevent sweating.

They also freeze well after blanching and will last this way for several months.

Broccoli:

Broccoli should be picked when the head is good and firm, and before it begins to flower. Even if the heads or florets are small, they should be cut away before the flowers begin to show otherwise they will become inedible.

Although broccoli can be grown throughout the season, they prefer the cooler climates and should even be harvested in the morning before the sun warms the ground up for best flavour.

It is best eaten within a few days of plucking, but will last for 2-3 weeks in the fridge or a cool place. To keep for longer, then blanch for a few minutes before freezing.

Broccoli will keep for up to 1 year frozen.

Cauliflower:

Cauliflower is another cool-season crop that dislikes temperatures over 60F.

When the head has fully formed (meaning that it is compact and white) and it is ready to harvest, cut at the base of the head with a sharp knife, leaving some leaves intact to protect the head.

If the head has a course rough appearance, or is discoloured then it should be disposed of. Small heads that have started to open should also be harvested immediately as they will soon open completely and be inedible.

It will keep in the refrigerator if wrapped in a polythene bag for about a week. To keep longer than this then it will have to be blanched and frozen.

Cauliflower also makes a good pickle, and will keep for several months in a pickle jar.

Cabbage:

Although cabbage is generally harvested and eaten before the Fall arrives, there are some winter cabbage varieties such as Huron, OS Cross and Danish Ball Head, that will last well into early winter.

These can be kept in the ground until ready to consume, so long as you are not in an area prone to severe frost or winter conditions that will result in the plant being burst and ruined.

If you do have to harvest to avoid the worst winter, then these cabbages are best kept in the cool environment of a root cellar.

There or in a refrigerator, they can last for several months stored on racks with a free flow of air around them.

Peas & Beans:

Now is the time to bring in the last of the pea and bean harvest – again depending on the varieties you have planted.

Peas and beans can be kept frozen for up to 12 months by simply removing them from the pods, then blanching for about 90 seconds in boiling water before cooling then freezing them.

Alternatively they can be dried out and stored for months to be used in soups and casseroles. This can be done either by leaving then on the plant to mature and dry out, or by removing the beans from the pod and laying them out in well ventilated place to dry completely.

If leaving on the vine to dry, then freeze for a minimum of 48 hours after harvesting to kill any bean weevils that may be present.

This process will kill the eggs, larvae and any adult weevil that may have infected the bean whilst on the plant.

Leeks Onions & Shallots:

Late onions and shallots should be pulled from the ground and left for a few days to dry out – unless of course the weather has turned wet in which case you should lay them out on racks indoors where it is cool and dry.

After the foliage has dried then they should be strung together and hung up somewhere cool, dry, and frost-free for the winter.

In this condition they will last for several months over winter, usually until the following springtime.

Leeks on the other hand like colder climates and can be left in the ground over winter, provided that you do not have a deep penetrating frost.

To protect them from deep frost, mulch over them with straw or dry grass up to 10 inches or so deep. They can then be lifted as and when they are needed.

To store above ground, they will keep in the fridge for about 1 week as they are lifted and cleaned. Alternatively cut the greenery away to about 1 inch above the white, leave the roots intact and store in box with damp sawdust or vermiculite.

Stand the plants upright and store away in a root cellar preferably, where it should be cool and moist. They will keep fresh for up to 8 weeks or so in this condition.

Root Vegetables:

Root vegetables are fairly versatile when it comes to harvesting, owing to the fact that they can often be left exactly where they are in the ground!

This is especially the case with parsnips and swedes which can benefit from a light touch of frost. If you are in an area that is prone to deep ground frost however they are best harvested and stored.

To 'store' them over winter in the ground, they must be treated pretty much the same way as the leeks in the previous chapter, with a protective covering of straw or mulching material.

Do not worry about a covering of snow, as this only acts as an insulator for ground-dwelling root vegetables.

If you are lifting them and storing them for the winter, then roots such as carrots, parsnips, swedes, potatoes and beets must be kept in a humid but well-ventilated frost-free area.

The high humidity (around 85-90%) acts to prevent the vegetables from drying out, giving that wrinkled look you so often see when veggies are stored inside.

The ventilation is to prevent the growth of fungal contaminants that would otherwise prosper is a damp environment.

There are several very effective ways to store your root vegetables, that will keep them fresh and crisp over the winter months ahead.

Vegetable Clamp:
This can be achieved in its simplest form by building a root clamp – otherwise known as a potato clamp as it is most often used for that vegetable.

A root clamp or mound, should be constructed on a slight raise in the ground if possible, on free-draining soil to prevent water from gathering amongst the vegetables.

A small 'moat' is formed around the mound and filled with crushed gravel to act as drainage. The Roots are laid out on a bed of straw, covered over with a 2-4 inch layer of straw, then covered over again with about 6 inches of garden soil (thicker if you have severe winters).
You will notice a bunch of straw poking out of the top?
This is to act as ventilation for the vegetables stored below.

Bin Cellar:

Many types of every-day articles can be buried under the ground and used to store your roots over winter. This is an example of a 'Bin cellar' a simple trash bin adapted to double as an effective root cellar.

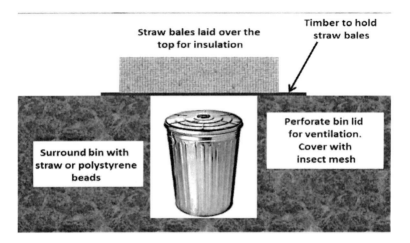

Basement Storage:

If you happen to have a basement or even a garden shed adapted to make it frost-free, then roots can be simply stored in shallow boxes or crates.

Before storing carrots, parsnips or beets; cut or twist away the foliage to about 1 inch from the top. Be careful especially with the beets that you do not damage the beet itself, or it is likely to 'bleed out.'

Lay out your box then add an inch or so of moist sand or sawdust, before laying out a layer of carrots or parsnips. Fill over with the moist filler before adding another layer of roots. Continue this process making sure that the vegetables do not touch.

Potatoes can be simply stored in a dark place in the corner, then covered over with hessian or paper sacks.

Permanent Root Cellar:
Of course the ideal solution for storing beets over-winter, and fruit, vegetables, and dairy products over the summer periods, is a full-blown Root Cellar!

The remit for building such a Cellar is a bit beyond the intentions of this short work on vegetable storage, however the basic principle is the same as that of the 'Bin' cellar in that you are aiming for a high relative humidity, a frost-free environment and good ventilation.

A very good book on the subject from my colleague Norman J Stone, is called Root Cellar Construction.

This book also includes detailed instructions on storing Root Vegetables, along with many other aspects of Root Cellar operation.

MY NOTES/THINGS TO DO

MY NOTES/THINGS TO DO

2: Pruning Fruit Trees & Bushes

Pruning the fruit trees or berry bushes is a job that should not take up a huge amount of your time (depending on how many trees you have I), however it is something that will reap great rewards over time.

Pruning is done for a number of reasons. It could be to cut away dead or unproductive wood, or to promote healthy growth in the coming spring.

Of course a fruit tree can be pruned to train it along a particular supporting frame-work, or even to shape the tree into some aesthetically pleasing shape.

Whatever the other reasons for pruning though, perhaps the most important is the former 2. To trim away dead, diseased, or broken branches and to promote healthy growth, and by doing so increase fruit yield and overall health of the tree.

With all that said however, fruit trees in general should not be pruned until the worst of the winter weather is over. The reason for this, is that pruning too early may put the tree under stress or encourage winter damage.

This of course applies to 'late' pruning. Trees can (and are) pruned throughout the growing season, but mainly during July and November - March.

Winter (or Dormant) pruning can also result in a burst of new growth in the spring, which in turn can lead to a lot of foliage on fast-growing upright shoots - but little fruit. This is due to the root system trying to feed the pre-pruned tree – in effect over-feeding it.

Pruning Cuts:

There are three basic cuts that are used in the tree pruning process, and these are as follows.

Heading Cut: This removes only the very end of the growing shoot, and promotes growth of both the lower buds and the buds just under the cut.

Bench Cut: This is a major cut and is used to remove vigorous upright shoots right back to the side branches. This cut is used to clear space in the middle of fruit trees, allowing sunlight into the central area.

Thinning Cut: This cut is used for general trimming and removes a vigorous shoot right back to the main side-shoot.

Always use a sharp knife or secateurs when pruning your fruit trees, and avoid tearing the branch away! This will cause damage to the tree and encourage insect or disease attack.

All cuts should be at an oblique angle to allow for the rapid dispersion of water from the cut. This will speed up the healing process, as will pruning compounds to seal the wound – not absolutely necessary, but they are an added precaution.

General Autumn Care: This involves clearing away any debris from around the plant to discourage winter-hibernating pests.

Protect the tree bark from nibbling mice by wrapping with a protective shield. Tie down any loose branches if training your fruit tree, to ensure no winter damage by wind or heavy snow.

Check that tree stakes are firm and upright, and the plant properly secured.

Fruit Berry Bushes:

Berry bushes need pruned regularly in pretty much the same way as fruit trees do, and for similar reasons.

Blackcurrants, red currents, and white currents are popular fruits for jam and jelly making. The blackcurrant in particular is a favourite amongst fruit berry growers for its versatility and rich juicy berries.

These should be cut back soon after fruiting during the early Autumn period.

Unlike red or whitecurrants which fruit on old wood; blackcurrants fruit on new wood. This means that for established plants the previous year's wood should be cut to about 1/3 its length, with any old or diseased growth cut out entirely..

New plants should be pruned by cutting all shoots back to two buds above ground level. This allows the root system to get more established and produces a healthier crop in the long term.

Established plants should have the main shoots cut back by about 1/3 each year, to prevent overcrowding which will increase the chances of fungal diseases. Shoots growing out sideways should be cut back or supported to prevent fruit from lying on the ground as the shoot becomes fruit-bearing.

White and Redcurrants: Bearing in mind that red & whitecurrants produce the fruit from old wood; pruning should be done by removing very old or diseased branches in the winter, leaving the healthy previous-years growth to produce fruit in the next growing season.

This is also the time to take cuttings from the bushes for the next season. Cuttings taken from established plants in November, can be cut to about ten inches long and heeled in (buried horizontally in a sandy trench and covered over) over winter.

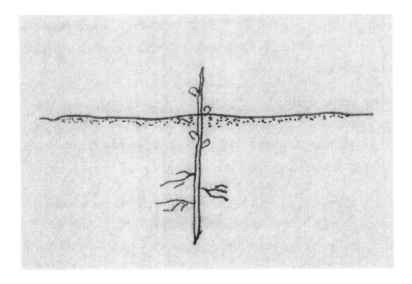

These cuttings can then be planted in march to form a new bush, by inserting 2/3 of the stem into the ground leaving the top three buds exposed.

Raspberries, Blackberries & Gooseberries:

One of the main areas of plant care with regard to these top berry bushes is pruning, and if done properly this will ensure high yields and a good crop of fruits for many years.

After the first crop of fruits and at the end of the growing season, ever-bearers can simply be cut down to the ground and left to grow for the next season. Other summer fruit varieties are pruned by snipping away the depleted fruit-bearing canes, and leaving the newer canes to produce fruit for the next season.

Black and purple raspberries produce fruit from side branches grown from the main cane. During summer cut away the main canes after they have fruited, but snip the tops of new canes at about 3 foot tall to encourage side growth throughout the growing season.

Pruning Gooseberries should be done in the late autumn by cutting back new growth to the first 2 buds, and the leaders to about 1/3 size.

Cut away any dead or damaged branches to open the center of the bush and allow for new growth.

MY NOTES/THINGS TO DO

3: Autumn Planting

Although the Autumn may be upon you and the fall has already started, in some areas there is still vegetables that can be planted for a late winter crop – this is especially so if you live in the warmer planting zones as indicated in the map below.

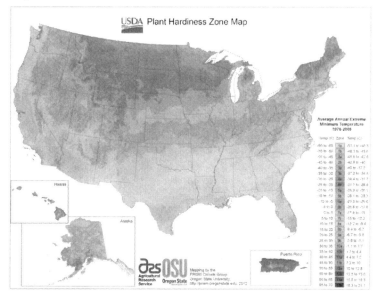

For a clearer picture of the individual average temperatures, the following diagram makes things a lot clearer. My apologies in advance to my readers from other parts of the world for only including the US figures here, a quick internet search is all it takes however, to get the hardiness zones for your own country of residence.

Average Annual Extreme Minimum Temperature 1976-2005

Temp (F)	Zone	Temp (C)
-60 to -55	1a	-51.1 to -48.3
-55 to -50	1b	-48.3 to -45.6
-50 to -45	2a	-45.6 to -42.8
-45 to -40	2b	-42.8 to -40
-40 to -35	3a	-40 to -37.2
-35 to -30	3b	-37.2 to -34.4
-30 to -25	4a	-34.4 to -31.7
-25 to -20	4b	-31.7 to -28.9
-20 to -15	5a	-28.9 to -26.1
-15 to -10	5b	-26.1 to -23.3
-10 to -5	6a	-23.3 to -20.6
-5 to 0	6b	-20.6 to -17.8
0 to 5	7a	-17.8 to -15
5 to 10	7b	-15 to -12.2
10 to 15	8a	-12.2 to -9.4
15 to 20	8b	-9.4 to -6.7
20 to 25	9a	-6.7 to -3.9
25 to 30	9b	-3.9 to -1.1
30 to 35	10a	-1.1 to 1.7
35 to 40	10b	1.7 to 4.4
40 to 45	11a	4.4 to 7.2
45 to 50	11b	7.2 to 10
50 to 55	12a	10 to 12.8
55 to 60	12b	12.8 to 15.6
60 to 65	13a	15.6 to 18.3
65 to 70	13b	18.3 to 21.1

Autumn Crucifers (Brassicas):
Planting in the fall is possible with brassicas in the more southerly regions, mainly however the Fall is harvest time for these tasty veggies.

This **includes broccoli, winter cabbage, brussels sprouts** and cauliflower, all of which can do well in the fall and produce fresh vegetables over the Christmas season.

Indeed they thrive in the cooler temperatures of Autumn, and as an added bonus you will not be fighting off the cabbage moth as you would do over the summer season!

Seedlings should be started in late summer for an Autumn harvest, about 3 months before the first frost of winter.

Radishes are also a good choice for late planting as they will mature from seed in about 30 days. They are also able to withstand a light frost.

Carrots and parsnip take around 65 days to mature, and can be left in the ground if protected from ground frost.

This can be done simply by covering with mulching material, straw, or fallen leaves.

Late Autumn varieties such as 'Autumn King' can be planted as late as August and be ready for harvest by late October.

Lettuce is fast growing (about 30 days from seed). Choose a loose leaf variety so you are able to cut away leaves as you need them, rather than wait for a full head to form.

Garlic: If you're a garlic lover then this can be planted in the late fall in many zones for a late spring-early summer harvest. Protect from the worst of the winter by covering with loose straw or mulch.

As an aside – garlic is an excellent companion plant for carrots, as the pungent smell distracts the carrot fly!

Cover Crops:
Rather than leave the ground bare and unproductive over the late season/winter, try planting out some cover crops such as ryegrass, winter rye, white clover, sweet clover, crimson clover, hairy vetch and buckwheat.

Planting cover crops is a highly efficient way of improving the soil structure as well as adding nutrients and preventing soil erosion during exceptionally dry or wet periods. Simply sow the seeds (usually before mid-August), and (after cutting if necessary) turn over the mature crops into the soil in the early spring.

Hardy Legumes such as Hairy vetch (Vicia villosa) make excellent nitrogen-fixing cover crops that provide organic matter as well as fertilizer. Sow in the Autumn and cut down before they flower in the early spring, then till them under.

Alternatively you can cover the growing area with leaf moult, or with the last of the summer grass cuttings. Leave to cover the area over winter, and turn into the ground before planting again in the springtime.

This is an efficient way to add humus and nutrients to the soil by using up the excess material that the Fall may produce.

Growing In Raised Beds?
Another thing to consider, is growing in raised beds. This extends your growing season, as the raised beds stay warmer for longer into the season.

This concept is particularly effective for root vegetables as the infill (if it has been done properly!) will be warm, loose and ideal for growing carrots and parsnips in particular.

If you have a poly-tunnel this also is perfect for growing later Autumn or early spring crops.

Storing Seeds/Planting Bulbs:
Collecting and storing your own seeds can save money and assure you of good crops in the next growing season. Tulip, crocus and daffodil bulbs can be planted at this time, not

only for a beautiful back-drop, but also as an addition to your companion planting efforts.

Store your seeds by laying out on a shelf until they have dried out completely, then place into a brown paper bag over winter. Remember to label the bag clearly. I don't know how many times I have neglected to do this, and suffered the consequences when the planting season was suddenly upon me!

You may have to keep them in a sealed container in order to keep them away from rodents that will otherwise treat them as a healthy snack!

4: Composting

Composting is another important task for the Autumn period. This is especially the case over the Fall as leaf moult and general clearing up of old vegetables etc, means that there is plenty of material for the compost pile.

With leaf moult in particular, bear in mind that dried leaves represent the 'brown' material or carbon content needed for your compost heap. Try not to over-do the volume of dried leaves therefore that you add to your compost pile.

The diagram below shows a typical compost layering system.

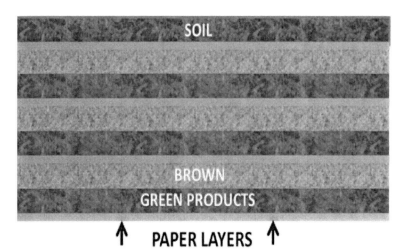

Pile up excess leaves elsewhere if possible to add to the compost pile as required, or use as in the 'cover compost' article above.

Maintaining or attending to your traditional compost heap is also important – especially if you are suddenly adding a whole load of new material to the compost.

The best way to do this is actually to construct (if you have not already done so) a proper composting area such as the one in the picture below.

This allows you to take better control of your composting efforts easily and effectively, by flipping your compost into the proper bins.

Left bin = Ready for use:
Middle bin = Almost done
Far right bin = Work in progress!

This particular composting bin series was made with wooden pallets picked up for free, and lined with chicken mesh for aeration and preventing the material from slipping through the slats.

In this instance a layer of weed fabric was laid down first, mainly because the area was atop an old stinging nettle bed with an abundance of deep roots. The last thing I want is the nettles to grow up through my precious compost!

This is not always necessary though, and in fact can be a bit of a pain when it comes to turning over the compost, as the fork quickly gets caught in the fabric.

Green Composting: This can be an effective method at this time of year, and this is achieved by using up the green waste your vegetable plot may have produced, not in the compost heap – but directly dug into the garden itself.

This will rot down over the winter and effectively add nutrients and humus to the soil. Simply dig a trench or ditch in the vegetable plot or growing area. Pile in a good mix of greenery, cuttings, garden waste etc; and cover over with soil.

Alternatively just scatter the material over the veggie patch in the late Autumn, and dig into the soil a couple of weeks before you are due to begin planting in the spring.

This is sometimes also called 'Cover Composting.'

5: Repair & Maintenance:

Before the cold weather really sets in, and your fingers cannot stand the cold for more than a few minutes, it is the ideal time to make any running repairs to your greenhouse and outbuilding, as well as garden tools both motorised or manually operated.

General Clear-out:
Autumn is the time to get busy with clearing out the old seed beds and turning over the ground, or planting a cover crop?

It's time also to clean up the greenhouse, potting shed, etc. Repair any old broken glass and see to any leaks. Oil the hinges and repair the latches on the opening windows.

Maybe time to consider a coat of paint or timber treatment, if you have a wooden greenhouse or cold-frame layout.

Clear out blocked gutters and down-pipes, as well as cleaning out the water butts if needed.

Any tools and equipment that is not likely to be needed for the work required over the late fall, such as grass-cutting; should be cleaned and serviced at this time ready for a clean start in the winter.

After cleaning garden shears and other cutting equipment especially, a quick spray with good release oil or even a wipe down with an oily rag will keep them in good shape over the winter.

Pond Clear-out:
Time to clear away the excess growth and leaf-litter from the garden pond or water source, if you have one. If not, then maybe it's something you should consider!

A pond is great for encouraging birds as well as slug-eating frogs, newts and toads into your garden. All of these creatures play a part in a healthy ecologically balanced garden.

Be careful if your pond has a synthetic liner that you do not pierce it with garden implements in your efforts to pull out the excessive growth.

Pond pumps may also have to be removed and taken indoors for the winter, depending on just how hard a frost you normally get. If the ice normally does no more than penetrate a couple of inches, then most pumps will be ok if left immersed over winter.

That said however, it will do no harm (and prolong the pump life) to remove the pump to clear out the filters and sort any potential problems before the coming spring.

Place a football or any floating object in the pond when the risk of ice is high. This can be removed to create a hole in the ice that allows pond-life such as hibernating frogs to come up for air.

Hammering solid ice to break it is not advisable, especially if you have fish in the pond – the shock waves can kill them, or at least cause distress.

<u>MY NOTES/THINGS TO DO</u>

MY NOTES/THINGS TO DO

Jam Recipes

Preparation & Tips:

Before launching into your jam-making, there are a few issues to deal with regarding general health and storage of your jams and jellies.

This will not only ensure your good health, but also the health and longevity of the jams you have so painstakingly produced.

An alternative to sterilising the jars by the method below, is simply to put them (including lids) into the dishwasher!

1: Jars must be properly and thoroughly cleaned (including the screw tops), with soapy water then added to a pre-heating an oven set to 130C (275F). Leave for about 20 minutes to sterilise.

2: Remove the jars from the oven with good oven gloves. Carefully add the jam to the jars while both are hot, otherwise you risk the jars shattering with the heat.

3: (optional with modern Jam jars) Leave the jam to cool, then add a cut disc of grease-proofed paper onto the surface of the jam, before screwing the lid down tightly. You can also buy waxed discs that are pre-cut, instead of the paper option.

More Tips..

As a general rule – DO NOT add hot food to cold jars or vice-versa, otherwise the glass is likely to shatter.

Unopened jams should be kept in a cool dry place, where they will last many months – 6 months at least. Once opened however it is best to consume within a month, and check regularly for any mould growth or other signs of spoilage.

Never fill your saucepan more than 1/3rd full, owing to the boiling jam more than doubling in volume as it boils.

A wax-disc or round piece of wax-proof paper placed on the surface of the jam after it is poured, is not as necessary as it used to be owing to the modern treatment of the inside of the lids – which used to rust.

Never use old pickle jars to store your Jam in if you can avoid it. If you do, then make sure you have thoroughly cleaned the lid especially, to remove the smell of vinegar.

Be sure to clean around the rim of the jar before screwing down the lid, to be sure that you will have an air-tight seal.

Scum will form on the surface of the jam as you are cooking, do not do anything with this until the process is complete and you have a set.

To remove the scum either scrape away the surface with a suitable spoon, or simply add a knob of butter and stir gently in. This should remove the scum by disintegrating it into the jam mix.

If mould does develop on the surface of the jam, simply remove the top 1/2 inch or so with a spoon, then cover with a wax disc dipped in brandy or bourbon to re-seal it.

Let your jam mixture cool for just a few minutes before pouring into the jars. This will avoid the fruits all floating to the top.

Here are some great Jam recipes to try for yourself, remember that all you have to do is substitute your own fruit in most cases, to get a recipe that suits your particular harvest or choice of Jam.

Raspberry Jam:

Ingredients:
1 kg (2.2lbs) Jam sugar (pectin added)
1 kg (2.2lbs) Raspberries
Juice of 1 lemon.

Begin by placing a saucer into the fridge to cool while you take the next step.

After thoroughly rinsing the berries and removing anything that should not be there! Tip half of the raspberries into a pan along with the lemon juice, mash with a potato masher and simmer for 5 minutes.

Place a fine sieve over a bowl and add the mixture, stirring with a wooden spoon so that all you are left with is the seeds.

Add the seed-free mix back into the pan along with the sugar and the other half of the raspberries. Boil rapidly for 5 minutes or so then remove a little of the jam and place onto the cold saucer.

The jam should wrinkle when you push your finger through it. If not then continue boiling and testing every 2 minutes until it does.

When this process is complete, pour carefully into the hot sterilised jars and immediately seal with a screw-on lid.

Blackcurrant & Apple Jam:

Ingredients:
500 gm (1.1lbs) Blackberries
500 gm (1.1lbs) Cooking apples, peeled, cored and chopped
Juice of 1 small lemon
1 kg sugar

Place a saucer in the fridge to chill, then add the blackberries, apples and lemon juice to a saucepan with 100ml (half cup) of water.

Simmer for 10-15 minutes until the fruit is tender and reduced. Add the sugar and boil vigorously for a further 5 minutes, making sure that the sugar has completely dissolved. Try the 'wrinkle test' as in the previous chapter by dropping some of the jam onto the cold saucer and testing.

If the Jam wrinkles then it is ready to pour into the jars. If not then boil for a further 2 minutes and test again. One of the advantages with using apples is that they contain a lot of natural pectin, which means that your jam should set quite readily.

The Jam can be poured into the hot jars, or poured into warm jars when it has cooled down slightly.

Store the Jam in a cool dry place, and when opened store in the fridge.

Gooseberry Jam:

Ingredients:
1kg (2.2lbs) Gooseberries
1 kg (2.2lbs) Granulated sugar
Juice of 1 lemon
400 ml (1.75 cups) water

After placing a saucer in the fridge to cool completely (for the wrinkle test). Place the gooseberries, water and lemon juice into a large saucepan, bring to the boil and gently simmer for about 15 minutes.

In a similar way to apples, gooseberries are high in pectin, so jam sugar should not be required.

Add the sugar and boil gently for a further 5-10 minutes until the sugar has completely dissolved. Turn up the heat and boil vigorously for a further 10 minutes, stirring regularly to prevent it sticking.

Place a drop of the jam onto your cold plate and leave a few moments. Lightly press your finger onto the cold jam and test to see if it wrinkles when prodded.

If not, then boil for a further few minutes and test again. Do this until your jam passes the wrinkle test. When it is ready pour into your HOT pre-prepared jam jars, making sure you fill them to just below the top, and seal the lid.

Jam should keep for 4-6 months at least in a cool dry place. Once open leave in the fridge where it should be consumed within 1 month.

Plum & Raspberry Jam:

Ingredients:
1 kg (2.2lbs) Jam Sugar
500 kg (1.1lbs) Raspberries
500kg (1.1lbs) chopped, stoned plums
Juice of 1 lemon
Zest of 1 orange
(makes approx 8 jars of Jam)

Before beginning, remember to place a saucer into the fridge to cool down for at least 15 minutes for your wrinkle test.

Add all the ingredients into a large saucepan, but leave out half of the raspberries. Heat slowly until all the sugar has dissolved, before bringing to the boil and simmering for a further 5 minutes.

Option – To reduce the raspberry seeds, then follow the instructions for seed removal on the raspberry jam recipe. After 5 minutes, add the rest of the raspberries and boil for a further 5-10 minutes. Take the pan off the heat and place some on the cold saucer for your wrinkle test.

If need be, then boil for a further 2-3 minutes, testing at the end of each time period. When Jam is ready, then carefully pour into your pre-prepared sterilised hot jars. Cover with wax disc and seal the lid down.
Follow previous instructions for storing your jam.

<u>MY NOTES/RECIPIES</u>

Apricot Jam:

Ingredients:
1 kg (2.2lbs) Apricots (chopped fine & stoned)
1 kg Jam sugar
Juice of 1 lemon.
1 cup (275ml) of water
I knob of butter
(makes approx 8 jars of Jam)

After preparing your jars and the cold plate as per the previous instructions. Place all the ingredients except the sugar and butter, into a suitable pan and bring to the boil. Simmer for a further 10-15 minutes until the fruit is softened.

Remove the pan from the heat and add the sugar and stir gently until dissolved, then add the butter and boil vigorously for a further 10 minutes.

Apply the wrinkle test to a spoonful of jam laid on a cold plate. Boil for a further 2-3 minutes if needed or until the jam passes the test.

When ready pour carefully into your pre-prepared jars, and after cleaning the rim, screw down the lid tightly.

Orange Marmalade:

(Can also be used with limes or lemons)

Ingredients:
1.25kg/2lb 12oz Seville oranges
1.5kg/3lb 5oz granulated sugar
4 pints of water
(makes approx 8 jars of marmalade)

After placing saucers in the fridge to cool as per the instruction for jam-making. Scrub the oranges thoroughly in warm to remove any wax (store-bought fruits such as oranges are often waxed to improve the look and longevity of the fruits).

Keep 3 oranges aside. Slice away the stem end of the remaining oranges, then chop into small cubes and place them into a deep pan, removing any pips. Take the three remaining oranges, slice away the stem end, cut in half and remove the skins.

Chop the remaining fruits up and add to the bowl. Slice the skins into fine strips and add to the bowl. Add the water and bring to the boil.

Let the mixture simmer for 45 minutes, then slowly add the sugar, stirring as you go. Let simmer for a further 10-15 minutes.

Perform the wrinkle test as in the previous jam recipes. When ready, pour into you pre-prepared hot jars and screw down the lids.

MY NOTES/RECIPIES

MY NOTES/RECIPIES

'Quick Canning' Pickle Recipes

Pickling is a great way to preserve excess produce from the garden, and to enjoy the fruits of your labour throughout the winter months.

The recipes in this section do not use the Canning 'Water bath' or 'Pressure Canning' methods which do in fact give a longer shelf life of up to 12 months. This compares to around 4 months for the 'quick canning' methods described below.

These pickling recipes offer a simpler approach to pickling your vegetables, most popular perhaps in the UK and throughout Europe in particular.

However it is essential that proper toughened preserving jars are used that will provide adequate seals and will not crack when exposed to heat.

Sterilisation measures are also essential to ensure against food spoiling and food poisoning!

Vinegar acts as a preservative and flavouring agent for most pickles, and there are 2 main types of vinegar used in this way.

Distilled white vinegar is the vinegar of choice for most folks as it is colorless and does not stain the vegetables. It is mellow in flavour and smell.

Apple Cider vinegar is a popular choice for many pickles as it has a mild fruity flavour that blends well with spices and fruits. It will however stain or darken many fruits and vegetables. **Always use vinegars with a 5% acetic acid content.**

Patience is a virtue – especially when it comes to pickles! Leave for **a few days at least** before consumption, otherwise they are likely to be strong and rather harsh tasting.

The best salt to use for pickles is sea salt, course, or cooking salt, as they do not have the additives that table salt has to prevent it from becoming lumpy.

Remember always to clearly label your jars with the date and product included.

Spices can be mixed to any of the pickling recipes, according to your tastes. It is common to add herbs, cinnamon sticks, garlic cloves or chillies to the vinegar brine if not already included in the particular recipe.

Here are some popular pickling recipes to try out for yourself.

Pickled Beetroot:

(good general mix for veg of many kinds including onions and gherkins)

Ingredients:
1 pound small beets (about 7 beets)
1/2 cup white vinegar
1/4 cup sugar
1/4 teaspoon salt

Scrub beets thoroughly but leave on roots and about 1 inch of stem. Place into a deep pan and cover with water. Bring to the boil and simmer for 45 minutes or until beets become tender.

Remove from the water, drain the water away and rinse the beets in cold water. When cool enough to handle, top and tail the beets, rub away the skins and slice into ¼ inch slices.

Alternatively, very small beets can be left whole. Pack the slices into hot sterilised Jars ready to be filled with the pickling liquid.

Add the vinegar, salt and sugar into a bowl, bring to the boil and stir until dissolved for about 5 minutes. Carefully pour the hot liquid into the jars filled with beetroots, then screw down the lids while still hot.

This can be done when the liquid is cool, but hot liquid will increase the longevity of your pickles. Leave to cool and add your labels with dates and descriptions.

MY NOTES/RECIPIES

Mixed Vegetable Pickle:

Ingredients:

2 lbs of pickling cucumbers. Washed and peeled then cut into short strips.

1lb peeled and quartered onions (small).

2 cups (16oz) chopped celery.

1 cup (8oz) peeled and chopped baby sweetcorn.

1 cup (8oz) sweet red peppers, chopped.

1 cup (8oz) small cauliflower flowerets.

5 cups white vinegar.

¼ cup of french grainy mustard.

1/2 cup canning or pickling salt

3-1/2 cups sugar

1/2 tsp whole cloves

1/2 tsp ground turmeric

Add the vinegar and mustard to a pot and stir till mixed well. Bring slowly to the boil adding the pickling salt, sugar, cloves and turmeric.

Add the vegetables and simmer for a further five minutes. Carefully add the mix to your pre-prepared HOT jars.

Clean the tops and screw on the lids. Leave for several days before using. Can be kept for 4 months or more in a cool dark place.

Pickled Green Beans:

Ingredients:

1 ½ lbs green beans trimmed to just below jar height.
½ teaspoon cayenne pepper.
2 garlic cloves peeled (optional).
2 teaspoons dill seeds.
2 cups white vinegar.
2 cups water.
½ cup canning salt.

Prepare jars by sterilising in hot water. Add the water, vinegar and salt to a pot then bring to the boil. Add the beans, garlic, pepper and dill seeds.

Simmer for 5 minutes. Carefully remove the beans and Pack them into the hot jars, then pour in the liquid to within ½ inch from the top of the jar.

Screw down the tops and leave to cool before labelling and packing away in a cool dark place for at least 5 days before use.

Pickled Jalapeno Peppers:

Ingredients:

1 pound jalapeno peppers, quartered.

1/2 pound sliced carrots.

1 small onion.

1 clove garlic, chopped.

1 tablespoon pickling salt.

1 teaspoon pepper.

3 cups white vinegar.

1 tablespoon extra-virgin olive oil.

2 table spoons sugar

3 table spoons salt

½ teaspoon of oregano

½ teaspoon of basil

1 pint water.

1 pint white vinegar.

After preparing your hot jars to receive the product. Pierce a small hole in each of the peppers to stop them collapsing, then add to a pot of water along with the sliced carrots. Bring to the boil and simmer for 5 minutes then remove and add them to the pickle jars.

Whilst the jalapenos are boiling, add the other ingredients into a pot and bring to the boil. Simmer for 5 minutes.

Pour the mixture into the hot jars containing your Jalapenos. Screw the lid down tight then let cool before labelling and storing in a cool dark place.

Leave for 5 days minimum before consumption to allow the flavours to infuse.

<u>MY NOTES/RECIPIES</u>

Pickled cauliflower:

Ingredients:
12 cups of small cauliflower flowerets
4 cups white vinegar
2 cups sugar
2 cups thinly sliced onions
2 tbsp french mustard seed
1 tbsp celery seed
1 tsp turmeric
1 tsp hot chili flakes

After preparing and sterilizing the jars as per previous instructions, blanch the cauliflower florets for 3-4 minutes in salt water before removing them from the pot and placing in cold water to stop cooking further.

Add the remaining ingredients into a pot and bring to the boil. Simmer for a further 2-3 minutes. Meanwhile add the cauliflower to the jars and when the mixture has finished simmering, add this also to the jars completely covering the cauliflower.

Seal down the lid and leave to cool before labeling and storing away.

Leave for a minimum 3-4 days before consumption.

MY NOTES/RECIPIES

MY NOTES/RECIPIES

Episode 2: Gardening Tips For Winter:

THE FOOD GROWERS TOP JOBS FOR THE WINTER SEASON.

Including Tasty Winter Soup Recipes!

BY

JAMES PARIS

Introduction:

Whilst seasonal gardening jobs to be undertaken pretty much depend on your global position and locality, gardening in one form or another is a year-round occupation for many keen gardeners.

In the USA the keen vegetable gardener in Florida can grow many veggies all year, while Wisconsin is covering up and preparing for the deep winter snows.

In the UK in general, apart from a few hardy winter crops such as brussels sprouts, winter cabbage, root vegetables etc that are harvested late in the season; vegetable planting pretty much grinds to a halt through the months from October to February.

In the cold North of Scotland especially, winter 'gardening' is restricted to survival of the fittest!

With all that said, this 'Winter Gardening' episode, will hopefully reveal a surprising amount of vegetable care that can be accomplished over even the coldest winter.

The keen gardener is always preparing for the next season, and the slow-down over the winter is the ideal time of the year to gather their thoughts and prepare for the coming planting season.

In this, the second episode of 'Seasonal Gardening Job's' for the vegetable gardener. The fall season is lapsing into full-blown winter, and hopefully you have done much of the preparation as highlighted in the first book in this series – 'Gardening Tips For Autumn'

Indeed many of the tasks included in that first book will be touched on again in this Winter season book, as many aspects of Autumn and Winter gardening overlap.

However it is now well into winter time and there is much to be done! Listed below is a brief outline of what you can expect to find in this book, as well as some of the things to prepare and get ready for the coming spring planting season.

Gardening tasks to be covered:

1. Planting late Autumn/Winter vegetables.

Provided you are not into the coldest winter or hardest frosts while reading this book, there are many vegetables that you can plant in preparation for a good late spring harvest.

In this section you will find a selection of the Top Ten vegetables to plant over this period. If you have access to a greenhouse or polytunnel, your options for harvesting some fresh vegetables in the early spring are excellent!

2. Protecting your winter vegetables.

Just because you are not actually planting over the coldest season of the year, does not necessarily mean that you have no vegetables to protect!

Root vegetables in particular can be left in the ground over winter in many areas, as long as they are protected from the frost.

Winter cabbage and other brassica have to be protected, and many other winter vegetables can be nurtured over the winter season.

3. Planning Ahead.

Winter is an excellent time for planning the layout and rotational stuff for next year's vegetable garden. Time to sit by a warm fire with a mulled wine maybe – and set out your garden for the coming spring.

This could include building a raised bed (why not?) or even planning a Straw Bale garden as an interesting experiment, if you have not attempted this before.

Paths and access to areas around the vegetable plot can be improved. As well as any rotten wooden edging or cold frames repaired ahead of the spring planting (if you're not using them over-winter that is).

4. Tools & Equipment.

Why is it that so many of us wait until the Rotavators or lawn mowers ceases to operate before we get them fixed! Winter is an excellent time to get the tools and equipment oiled and fixed, ready for use.

5. Misc Winter Gardening Tasks.

Here you will find a variety of winter tasks to be done whilst you have the time! Notwithstanding the shorter daylight hours, this is an excellent time to get a number of tasks done from pruning to transplanting.

There's also water taps to be lagged and compost heaps to get sorted. Fencing to repair and garden hoses to put away.

Oh…and remember the stock up the bird-feeders! The Robins and finches will hang around for the food, and pay you back by eating your caterpillar's in the springtime. It's called 'Quid pro quo' bro :)

<u>MY NOTES/THINGS TO DO</u>

Plant Hardiness Zone Maps

It's handy to know what zone you are in if you are to effectively plan your vegetable growing – no matter what the season.

Here are zone maps covering the USA and United Kingdom. My apologies if you are reading this from elsewhere, but I cannot include every country in this short work unfortunately.

The good news however is that you can easily do a quick search online and get all the zone maps you need instantly. In fact The following link gives a good selection of world plant hardiness maps.. http://www.edible-landscape-design.com/plant-hardiness-zone.html

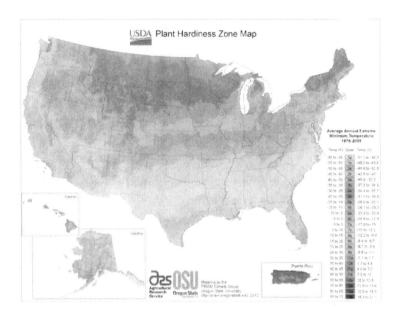

What zone you find yourself in pretty much determines what you are able to plant successfully, or indeed store in the ground effectively over the late Autumn or winter months (more on this later).

1:Winter/Autumn Vegetables

When we talk about growing winter vegetables, it has to be made clear that unless you live in warmer climes then we are really talking about planting in the early fall, and reaping the benefits as the early winter progresses.

Alternatively they can be planted in the late spring, usually a couple of weeks before the last frosts, to be ready for harvesting before the warmer weather arrives.

The bottom line is that once temperatures start to drop below 35F then even hardy cool season seeds will not germinate.

Once the plant has germinated and is growing however, then it is a case of protecting it from sudden drops in temperature – especially in the evenings.

The two main categories of **cool season** vegetables we are talking about here are Hardy vegetables and semi-hardy vegetables.

All cool season crops taste better when they mature in the cooler weather , and are therefore best suited to planting in the late summer or early spring seasons.

Between them they will thrive in growing temperatures from 40F to 60F ideally. Warmer climates will generally cause them to bolt and become inedible, this is the case of beets and swedes especially.

Hardy Vegetables include - broccoli, cabbage, kohlrabi, onions, lettuce, leeks, peas, radish, spinach, turnips.

These veggies will grow in temperatures as low as 35-40F and will survive a light frost, especially if protected by a garden fleece covering.

Semi-Hardy Vegetables include - beets, carrots, cauliflower, parsley, parsnips, potatoes, and Swiss chard.

This type prefer temperatures above 45-50F but below 75-80F and are susceptible to very cold or frosty conditions.

It is not only the temperatures that restrict winter growth however, the shorter winter daylight hours mean that the plants may not get the minimum of 6 hours daylight required in most cases for garden vegetables.

The growing season of all vegetables and not just Hardy types can be extended considerably by the use of cold-frames, and polytunnels that will protect the plants against the worst of the winter weather.

Hot Bed Gardening:

Although regarded by some as a 'new' concept in gardening methods (Is there such a thing?), this is an idea that goes way back in time – at least to the Roman conquest of Great Britain.

To supply the Roman generals with fresh salad in the frozen winters of Britain, was a challenge that the Roman gardeners of the time solved by using this method to supply fresh salad crops out of season – and probably stopped themselves getting flogged at the same time!

The French perfected this method in the early 1900's, and the Victorians used it to grow pineapples!

So what is it? A Hot Bed is basically an area heated by natural or artificial means to grow vegetables that would otherwise not grow owing to the cold temperatures.

There are quite a few ways to go about creating your own hot bed, here is one possible plan for a *natural* Hot Bed.

To create a simple Hot Bed garden you have to dig a trench 18-14 inches deep (450-600mm), then fill it with manure mixed with straw that has been piled up for 7-10 days beforehand. This is to allow a cooling down period otherwise the excess heat generated can kill the plants.

Once you have done this then place a cold-frame on top similar to the one below, and add 6 inches (600mm) good quality growing medium on top.

The heat generated will warm the soil, and the cold-frame arrangement will trap this heat nicely to allow growth and prevent frost in the cold season.

This natural method of Hot Bed gardening will on average last for about 3-4 months before the heat-producing aspect of the manure finishes.

The heat produced during this time should easily be in the region of 45-55F (8-13C) which puts it in the ideal range for the veggies listed below.

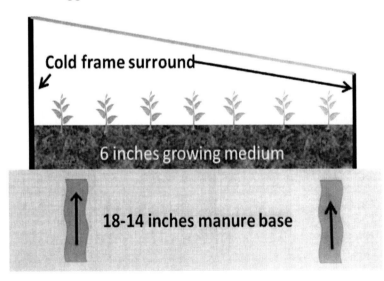

Another alternative to this natural method is to utilise an under-soil electric blanket, or electric cables to warm the growing medium.

This will be more expensive to operate (unless you produce your own electricity?), however it is easier regulated and you will have heat for as long as you pay your electric bills :)

In general terms this method is used around January so that the timing is right for the early spring gardening. By March the effectiveness of the heating-up process has virtually gone (in the natural method), and 'normal' spring gardening practices take over.

The good news is that you now have a nitrogen rich bed in which to grow a good variety of spring-summer vegetables (perhaps by removing the cold frame).

This may all seem like a load of extra work, however it is well worth considering if you are keen to keep your fresh vegetable supply going for as long as possible – even over the cold winter months.

You can also try a much simpler version by digging out the ground as above, but placing over it a mini-polytunnel to grow your veggies under.

Planting Times:

When planting seedlings or from seed itself, it is important to consider the time it takes for the plant to reach maturity, or at least to become harvestable. For instance planting too late in the Fall may mean that the plant will not reach maturity before the winter really closes in.

Planting beets or swedes too late in the springtime may mean that the hotter weather will cause the plants to bolt and become inedible.

With that in mind, the growing times and required ground temperatures, have to be considered when planning ahead for winter storage.

Another point to consider is whether or not you will be growing your vegetables under cover. As mentioned earlier, the use of a greenhouse, polytunnel, or cold-frame can mean that you are able to grow quite effectively in otherwise vegetable-intolerant conditions.

A polytunnel for instance that has perhaps been used to grow tomatoes during summer in cold northern regions, can be put to great use by growing a whole range of cool season vegetables.

Growing in Raised Beds is also an effective way to increase the growing season, as the Raised Bed tends to warm up quicker as it is lifted up from the cold ground temperatures of winter.

Combine the two and you have a marriage made in veggie heaven :)

MY NOTES/THINGS TO DO

2: Protecting Winter Vegetables.

Keeping your winter vegetables protected from the worst of the weather, is a no-brainer – especially after you have gone to all the bother planting them in the first place!

As mentioned earlier, this is considerably easier if you are growing your winter vegetables inside a polytunnel, cold-frame, or otherwise under cover.

Even in a polytunnel however, if the temperature drops below freezing it is advisable to cover your veggies with a gardeners fleece to protect against frost damage.

With vegetables growing outdoors, there are a number of precautions you can take to protect them from the worst of the weather.

1. For Parsnips and other root vegetables, providing the temperature does not fall below 23F (-5c) then they can effectively be left in the ground and covered over with a mulch of leaves or straw to a depth of around 6 inches.

There can be a downside to this method however, and that is that destructive pests and grubs can also use this method to over-winter in your veggie plot!

I overcome this problem by the following method. Wait till a few weeks before your last winter frosts, then (presuming you have harvested your vegetables by now) rake away the leaves and turn over the soil below with a garden fork.

This exposes any grubs and pests to the last of the frost and kills them. Alternatively, during this digging-over process you can include the leaf mulch into the soil, rather than removing it to add much-needed organic material.

This will not add much in the way of nutrients, as leaves are mainly carbon, but will improve the soil medium overall.

Do not worry too much about snow conditions, as snow acts as an insulator in most cases – protecting the veggies below. However if you are in an area that has severe penetrating ground frost, then it is best to harvest your root vegetables and store in a root cellar.

Alternatively store them in a sand-filled box in a garage or frost-free outbuilding.

Check out the diagram below for an example of a DIY ground-based root cellar.

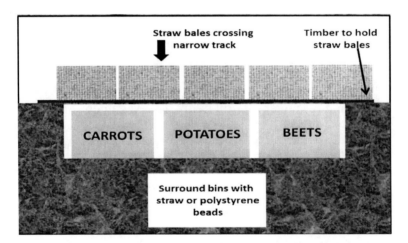

2. Garden fleece will protect your cool season vegetables such as broccoli, salad crops, or winter cabbage against frost damage. Fleece or netting will also protect them from the ravages of pigeons!

Even an old blanket or hessian sacking thrown over the veggies at night, will protect them from the night-time drop in temperature – just remember to remove it again in the daytime.

3. Leeks can be lifted before the ground is frozen and 'heeled in' to a trench that is sheltered from the worst weather. They will last several months over winter in this situation.

4. Vermin can do a lot of damage to vegetable crops left in the ground over winter – especially if the weather is particularly bad and food is at a premium.

A couple of years ago I lost a good parsnip crop that had been growing in pots & containers to a family of rats!

They dug the parsnips right down the length of the root to get every last morsel – I was gutted, as was my wife who had been looking forward to honeyed parsnips for the Christmas dinner!

Needless to say the rats were promptly dealt with, however I had to buy the Christmas parsnips. Use whatever means at your disposal to deny them access, including ½ inch chicken mesh if need be, to be sure your roots are protected against mice and rats over the winter period.

Rats in particular are opportunists, and will nest near a food source if they can find one. Make sure there are no easy places for them to set up home such as piles of junk or other rubbish.

Check out the compost heap regularly, as they will dig into the compost or piles of manure, for both the food source and the heat over winter months.

5. Build a cheap Polytunnel! This is not as hard as it might seem, and can be quickly achieved simply by bending plastic plumbers pipe into loops, and sticking the ends down into the soil.

Cover over with clear polythene, held down by soil along the length of the construction, and you have an instant – albeit a bit flimsy – polytunnel that will protect your plants admirably.

A Raised Bed vegetable garden offers even better possibilities as you can see from the picture below.

Just replace the insect mesh with either garden fleece or polythene to have a fully protected growing area for your Autumn/Winter vegetables.

Fresh winter vegetables can offer a valuable and nutritious change to dried or frozen vegetables. And even though you may certainly be restricted as to the choices open to you, there is no doubt that winter need not be completely unproductive when it comes to fresh veggies for the table.

3: Planning Ahead

A truly successful gardener is one that is constantly planning ahead, not only for the next season, but also how to lay out the garden plot to get the best out of it, whether for vegetable production, flowers or just the aesthetics of the area.

For the vegetable gardener especially, this is a time to get out the pencil and paper. Or the pc, notebook, iPad or whatever!

Snowy cold winter days are an ideal time to relax by an good fire with a hot drink, and get your plans and schemes set out for the coming season.

Draw out a plan for your planting to be sure that the plants are properly rotated. This is essential to ensure you are not stripping out all the nutrients needed for the plants you plan to grow.

Consider companion planting requirements in order to restrict or even cut out entirely your need for chemical fertilizers or pesticides, whilst at the same time improving your crop yield.

Take note of areas where you may perhaps be planning a Raised Bed garden, and get to work sketching your ideas down or even constructing the frames themselves.

This is a great time to consider changing the entire layout of your vegetable garden, if improvements can be made in order to improve production or overall usability!

MY NOTES/THINGS TO DO

VEGGIES	GOOD COMPANION	BAD COMPANION
Asparagus	Tomato, Parsley, Basil	
Beans	Beetroot, cabbage, celery, carrot, cucumber, corn, squash, pea's, potatoes, radish, strawberry.	garlic, shallot or onions
Beets	broccoli, brussels sprouts, bush beans, cabbage, cauliflower	charlock, field mustard, pole beans
Cabbage	cucumber, lettuce, potato, onion, spinach, celery.	strawberries
Carrots	beans, peas, onions, lettuce, tomato, leeks, and radish	Dill
Celery	Bean, tomato and cabbage family	Corn, Irish potato and aster flowers
Corn	Potato, pumpkin, squash, tomato, cucumber	tomatoes
Cucumber	cabbage, beans, cucumber, radish, tomato	late potatoes
Eggplant	beans, peas, spinach, tarragon, thyme	
Garlic	cabbage, cane fruits, fruit trees, tomatoes	peas, beans
Lettuce	Cabbage, carrot, beet, onion, and strawberry	cabbage family
Melon	pumpkin, radish, corn, and squash	
Onions	cabbage family, beet, tomato, pepper, strawberry, peas, and chard	beans, peas
Parsley	asparagus, carrot, tomato and corn	mint
Peas	beans, carrot, corn and radish	garlic leeks, onions, shallots
Peppers	Tomato, eggplant, carrot and onion	fennel, kohlrabi
Potatoes	bean, cabbage, squash and peas	apples, cherries, cucumbers, pumpkins, sunflowers, tomatoes
Pumpkin	Melon eggplant and corn	Potato, raspberry
Radish	carrot, cucumber, bean, pea, melon	hyssop
Squash	melon, pumpkin, tomato, beans, cucumber, onion	Potato, tomato
Strawberry	bean, lettuce, onion and spinach	Cabbage, broccoli, Brussels sprouts
Tomatoes	celery, cucumber, asparagus, parsley, pepper and carrot	fennel, kohlrabi, potatoes

Paths can be established and areas cleared much easier in the winter (as long as the ground is not frozen or knee-deep in snow!) as you do not have an abundance of weeds to contend with.

Seed and Bulb Orders. This is also an ideal time to get out the gardening catalogues and order up your seeds or bulbs. Ordering online early, means that you will not miss the growing season with orders arriving late.

Do you suffer from water-logged or boggy ground? Now is the time to plan and execute a drainage program that will enable you to convert useless land into good growing land for the next season.

4: Tools & Equipment

Keeping the garden equipment in good shape is not always easy over a busy growing season. However this is an ideal winter task that will reap benefits in later months.

Before packing away your lawn mower for the winter, be sure to clear out the old grass and muck that is stuck under it! If left in place this will only help corrode away the machine and shorten its lifetime.

Clean off your tools, especially secateurs and shears, pruners and loppers. Remove muck and rust then wipe them over with an oily rag. Do this before hanging up or packing away for the winter and you will be ready to go, perhaps after a quick sharpening in the spring.

Spades, shovels, garden forks etc should have the handles in particular checked and fixed if need be, before cleaning and hanging up to store.

Wheelbarrows should be cleaned, wheels oiled, and stacked under shelter – not left to fill with water or debris over the winter – oh yes...I've been there!

Pots and containers, particularly if you plan on doing container gardening in the spring, should be gathered up, cleaned out, and stacked away.

If you have unglazed clay pots in particular, then be sure to pack them under cover away from potential frost damage. Otherwise when you go to use them in the spring, they are likely to be cracked and useless.

Electric tools should have all the plugs, cables, and connections checked. Repair or replace where necessary any cables that have split, corroded or indeed been cut – the hedge trimmer is usually a favourite for this :)

Always be sure to use an exterior RCD (residual circuit device) when using electrical tools outdoors. This will immediately cut the power - should you accidently cut the cable!

5: Misc Winter Tasks

Even if you are not actively gardening as such, there are numerous other tasks you can get involved in to prepare for the coming spring – and to stop boredom from setting in!

<u>Pruning fruit trees</u> and shrubs, although some do this over the winter period, I would advise against this practice particularly if you are in an area prone to hard frosts.

If this is the case then pruning can result in frost-damage to the newly pruned part of the tree. Far better to prune trees and shrubs in late Autumn or Spring, after the last of the winter frosts.

Transplanting of fruit trees can certainly be done over the milder winter period, preferably late Autumn. This will give time for the roots to be established for the spring growth.

Pruning back can then be done as the spring growth starts to appear, and after the last frosts. Check regularly to make sure that the frost has not lifted newly planted shrubs. Press down the ground immediately surrounding them if this is so.

Winter digging-in in order to expose the open ground (and the bugs) to the winter elements is something that is still widely practiced.

However if you are on sloping ground it is not advised so much, as it means that the nutrients in the soil are free to run-off after heavy rain or snow melt.

In this instance it is better to wait until just before the last frosts of winter before digging over and preparing for the spring planting.

Digging-in well-rotted compost or manure at this time will prepare the ground well for the spring growing or flowers or vegetable crops.

Ponds should have an area kept clear of ice by placing a football or some other floating object in whilst it remains unfrozen.

Removing this later will create a clear area for aquatics such as fish and over-wintering frogs and toads to breath. Do not smash the ice with a heavy hammer if you can avoid this as it is likely to concuss and kill fish in particular.

Fill the bird feeders! Keeping your local bird-life well fed will help ensure their survival over a bleak winter, and help persuade them to stay around for the spring. This will ensure you have a healthy bird population to help you out with keeping destructive insects at bay.

Garden hoses should be drained before being neatly rolled and stacked away for the winter. Leaving the sprinklers or other fittings attached at the end of the hose is a bad mistake, as they will likely freeze and burst if there is still water in them.

Make sure you have adequate lagging on outside taps and pipes to prevent freezing. The outside tap water supply should be turned off and the taps themselves left open to prevent ice forming and splitting the fittings.

Fences and sheds that need to be repaired is a cold but essential part of the winter tasks to be done. Best however before the cold weather really closes in, as frozen fingers do not hold nails so well!

This is also a time to repair any broken timbers and clean out the old material from garden plots as well as Raised Beds and containers.

Composting. Time to turn over the composting heap. Add new materials and generally see to it that the composting bins are in good shape.

If you do not already have one, then a good composting bin arrangement will pay dividends for years for very little expense. Here is an example of a triple bin composter made from old pallets.

This is an ideal system for rotating your compost. In the above example you will see Left to Right, mature compost, semi-mature and new on the far right.

This way, as the composting material in the middle bin rots down to a usable level you can transfer it to the left hand bin. This means that with proper management you can have excellent composting material on hand on a near-constant basis.

Snow Shovels, ploughs or whatever you need, have to be looked out and ready to hand – before the snow comes! The wrong time to source this equipment is when you actually need it – because everybody has the same idea and you are likely to find supplies gone!

Storm Damage particularly to polytunnels that may have suffered badly, needs to be addressed before the coming spring. Indeed if you are planning winter crops then repairs must begin immediately in this case!

Polytunnels can take a real battering in strong winds, so much so that many commercial growers remove the polythene over the winter if they are not actively using them.

Make sure that you position your polytunnel where it will get the best protection from the elements, as well as the most direct sunlight.

MY NOTES/THINGS TO DO

MY NOTES/THINGS TO DO

Soup Recipes

Spicy Root Vegetable Soup
(Serves 6-8 people)

This is a family favourite, with an oriental spicy flavour.

Ingredients:

1 Large butternut squash
2 large diced onions
1 ¼ lb (567g kg) carrots
1 ¼ lb (567g) parsnips
½ small swede/turnip
2 Large sweet potatoes
1 tsp curry powder/paste
½ teaspoon garam masala
¼ tsp chilli powder
¼ tsp ginger powder
2oz (56g) butter
4 pints (1.89 ltrs) of ham stock (or water with 4 ham stock cubes)
Splash of cooking oil (prevents butter from burning)

Preparation:

Dice all the vegetables into roughly 1" cubes.

Heat butter and oil in a large pot until melted, add the diced onions and spices. Fry for approx 1 minute stirring constantly.
Add the diced butternut squash and parsnips; fry gently for about 5 minutes.

Add the diced carrots, sweet potato and swede with the liquid stock. Put lid on pot and boil slowly until vegetables are tender which is usually about 25 minutes.

Remove and let cool; season with salt and black pepper then 'blitz' with a hand blender until smooth.
Re-heat for use.
Garnish with chives or a sprig of parsley.

This excellent soup freezes well, and ham stock can be replaced with a vegetable stock for vegetarian use.

Carrot and Sweet Potato Soup
(Serves 4)

Ingredients:

1 lb (454g) of carrots
1 lb (454g) sweet potatoes
2 pints (0.94 ltrs) ham or lamb stock
1 cup orange juice or juice of three oranges
Black pepper
¼ tsp of ginger powder
1 diced peeled apple
1 oz butter with a little cooking oil to prevent burning
1 finely chopped onion

Preparation:

Dice or chop vegetables.

Heat butter, ginger and chopped onion until butter is melted and the onion has taken on an opaque look – do not brown. Add stock, diced carrots, sweet potato, apple and orange juice to large enough pot. Add salt and pepper to season and boil for around 20 minutes or until the vegetables are soft.

Remove from heat and allow to cool. Blitz with a food processor or hand blender until smooth.

Re-heat to serve.

Freezes well.

Potato & Vegetable Soup

(Serves 6-8)

Great soup for a cold winters day!

Ingredients:

1 lb (454g) carrots
¾ lb (340g)parsnips
1 leek (chopped)
¼ swede/turnip
5 large potatoes
1 large onion
½ tbl spoon dried mixed herbs
Lamb shank
2 pints (0.94 ltrs) water

Preparation:

Clean and dice half of the carrots, parsnips, and turnip.
Grate the other half.
Dice the onion and chop the potatoes into reasonable sized cubes.

Fill a large pot with the water, and add the diced onion and the lamb shank along with the herbs; with salt and black pepper to taste.
Add the diced and grated vegetables, including the chopped leek.

Bring to the boil for approx 60 minutes, then remove the lamb shank. Separate the meat from the lamb shank, chopping up into pieces; then return the meat to the soup.

Freezes well.

Potato & Leek Soup

(Serves 6-8)

Ingredients:

3.5 lb (1.58 kg) of potatoes (chopped)
2 large leeks (chopped)
1 onion (diced)
1 large carrot (chopped)
2.5 pints (1.18 ltrs) chicken or vegetable stock
½ tbl spoon crushed black pepper

Preparation:

Add the chicken stock to a suitable pan, bring to the boil whilst adding the chopped potatoes, carrots, leeks and diced onions.

Add salt and pepper to season and flavour. Boil for approx 25 minutes, or until the potatoes are beginning to soften.

Cream of Cauliflower Soup

(Serves 6-8)

This is a truly fantastic creamy smooth soup that has proved to be a huge hit with my dinner guests – even those that do not like cauliflower!

Ingredients:

2 cauliflower heads
2 large potatoes
1 large onion
2.5 pints (1.18 ltrs) chicken stock
10 fl oz (0.29 ltr) double cream
¼ tbls black or white pepper
½ tbls French mustard
½ tbls celery salt
1 glass white wine
Parsley

Preparation:

Into a large pot add the chicken stock, pepper, mustard and celery salt.
Roughly chop cauliflower heads, potatoes and add to the mix. Finely chop the onion and add to the pan. Boil for approx 40 minutes.

Allow to cool, then blitz with a blender or food processor. Re-heat and add cream before serving, mixing thoroughly. Garnish with a sprig of parsley.

Freezes well, but do not add cream before freezing.

Slow Cooker Chicken Broth
(Serves 4-6)

Ingredients:
2 chicken thighs
1 chopped onion
5 oz (141g) dried broth mix
2 carrots (chopped)
2 pints (0.94 ltr) chicken stock
1 tsp mixed herbs
1 table spoon olive oil
Garnish of parsley
½ oz butter
Salt & black pepper to taste

Preparation:
Leave the broth mix to soak overnight in a bowl of water, then drain and add to the slow cooker.

Add the oil, butter and chicken into a hot saucepan. Fry until the chicken begins to brown, then remove and place into the slow cooker with the mix.

Fry the onion in the saucepan (after removing excess oil/fat) until softened, then add the chicken stock and the other ingredients.

Cook on 'low' for 6-8 hours, then remove the chicken pieces; place on a chopping board and carefully remove the chicken from the bone.

Chop the boned chicken into bite-sized pieces and place back into the soup; seasoning with plenty salt and pepper to season. Garnish with a little parsley sprinkled on top.

MY NOTES/RECIPIES

MY NOTES/RECIPIES

MY NOTES/RECIPIES

Episode 3: Gardening Tips For Spring:

THE FOOD GROWERS TOP JOBS FOR THE SPRING PLANTING SEASON.

BY

JAMES PARIS

Blog: www.planterspost.com

Introduction:

If you stay in a country where seasons are very pronounced, then the Spring season is perhaps the busiest part of the year for all gardeners whether of flowers, fruit or vegetables.

All the planning and preparation you have committed to over the cold dark winter days & nights, is now put into operation and it is time to "let the madness begin" In the garden.

However it is easy to get a little over-enthusiastic, and forget that late spring frosts can kill many plants that have been planted too early or been left unprotected (shame on you :)).

This means that quite apart from the actual planting, there is a lot to do if your veggies are to survive these late frosts, or indeed the warm dry weather that is about to come.

Beds have to be prepared. Methods such as Raised Beds or Containers. Even Straw or Hay Bales, have to be set-up and perhaps primed (as in the case of bales), ready to accept your seedlings or seeds.

Growing vegetables in particular, is all about reaping a harvest when the time is right. And the aim of any gardener should be to get the best 'value for money' with regard to actual money and time spent preparing for this harvest.

The satisfaction to be gained from pulling your own healthy carrots from the ground, or plucking juicy beefsteak tomatoes from the vine, some would say is almost beyond price.

And the health benefits to be gained from growing and feeding the family with your own home-grown vegetables goes far beyond mere nutrition. Something about growing things and having our hands in the soil has been proven to be very beneficial to our mental and spiritual well-being.

The garden is not just a place for growing plants, it is also a place for nurturing our spirits and soothing our troubles – unless our cabbages are being attacked by the cabbage moth!

Joking apart, Thomas Jefferson said it well when he remarked…*"No occupation is so delightful to me as the culture of the earth, and no culture comparable to that of the garden."*

Spring is here – Let the madness begin!

Gardening tasks to be covered:

1: Preparing The Ground

This involves getting the areas prepared for planting out the seeds or seedlings for an early start to the season. This could be Building or repairing Cold-Frames, Raised Beds or areas where you will be setting out your Straw Bale garden for instance.

Much of this work may already have been done, especially if your winter has been mild, or you have read and followed the plans in my Winter Gardening tips book! Yes, anyway, there is much to do if the growing season is to start with a bang and the kitchen is to be stocked up with early season fresh produce.

If you live in the colder northern climates particularly, then getting cold-frames, cloches or polytunnels organised is essential if you want to get that early start.

Polytunnels:
In the case of Polytunnels in particular, the winter winds can cause havoc especially if the covering is getting older and perhaps a bit brittle – as was the case with the Polytunnel in the picture below!

Fortunately in this case the metal frame-work was still in good condition, so I was able to get it back in service again with some willing hands.

If you are unfamiliar with the construction of these things. This simply meant that I had to dig a channel along each side of the framework (on the outside), to release the old Polythene which is held in place by the weight of the soil covering.

With the trench dug out and the old material removed, we then straightened up the frame and threw over the covering. After this has been inserted into the trench on one side, it is covered over with soil and tamped down.

The cover is then sunk into the opposite side and pulled down tight on the frame as it is being covered over, and the trench filled in.

The ends are pulled around and fixed to the wooden door-frame or pulled down and into a trench around the end of the Polytunnel.

These simple and relatively cheap constructions offer a whole range of possibilities for growing a good selection of early and late vegetables.

Once you have it all erected properly the addition of a Hot Bed along one side can give you a fantastic early start to your vegetable growing if you choose this option.

This in fact gives you two advantages as the Hot Bed will not only allow you and early start, but it may also serve to raise the temperature within the Polytunnel sufficiently to keep frost at bay. This in turn means that other plants within the polytunnel will also benefit from an early start to the season.

What Is A Hot Bed?

This subject is covered fairly extensively in two previous books I have on the subject (Hot Bed Gardening and Winter gardening Tips) – links to which can be found above – so in case I am accused of 'padding out' here, I will keep it brief :)

In essence a Hot Bed is simply a growing area that is artificially heated by either organic or other means to allow for early planting of spring vegetables, or growing in temperatures that would normally be too cold for the intended plant.

There are many ways to create your own natural or organic Hot Bed, the most familiar being the cold-frame hot bed garden.

Simply dig a pit 18-14 inches deep and roughly the same outside dimensions of your cold-frame. Fill this up to 6 inches from the top with horse manure preferably, though the manure from sheep, cows, goats and chickens will suffice.

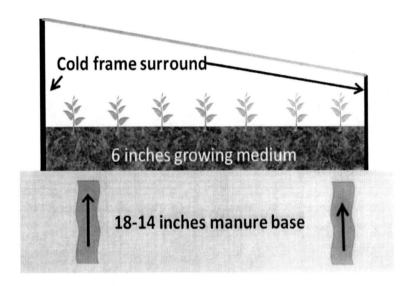

Trample it down, give it a good soaking and then add 6 inches of good soil or growing medium. Leave for about 10-14 days to cool slightly before planting your seeds or young plants

The end result of this is that the rotting manure creates heat under the soil which should last for between 2-3 months, effectively meaning that you can plant much earlier in the season as soon as the daylight hours begin to extend sufficiently for your plants to thrive.

Other ways to create a Hot Bed include using electrical cables especially designed for the purpose. Hot water pipes or warm air channels can also be used most effectively.

Though generally more expensive to operate these methods to offer advantages in respect to heat control and also longevity of the process, as they are not restricted by the natural processes of a manure Hot Bed.

Cold Frames & Cloches

This is also a time to get the cold-frames cleared out and prepared to accept your young plants or seeds. Remember not to be too enthusiastic when it comes to sowing seeds early on in the Spring!

A late frost can soon reduce your efforts to nothing – especially if you have forgotten to cover them over at night with garden fleece or even loose dry straw to protect them.

Our local garden centre makes a fortune by selling early plants to over-keen gardeners, who don't realise that they have been forced-on in heated polytunnels. They soon perish when planted out-with these ideal conditions – meaning that the plants have to be bought again!

Cold Frames and cloches do not have to be great works of construction. Simply make a frame raised on one side to catch the early sun, and cover over with an old window or sheet of polypropylene to cover the plants.

Originally a glass bell shaped structure much loved by the Victorians, a modern-day cloche is usually a simple structure to cover rows of seedlings – like a mini-polytunnel. This can be made from wire hoops or from plumbers plastic pipe stuck into the ground so that a tunnel is formed.

Also referred to as 'row cover.' These simple structures can also be covered with insect mesh in the summer to protect your brassicas from the cabbage moth and other flying pests.

Cloches come in all shapes and sizes depending on the requirement and also on the pure aesthetics but there goal is the same – plant protection and propagation.

These hoop cloches can be simply made by constructing a frame using 3 x 2 timbers and attaching the plumbers plastic pipe either in holes drilled on top – as in the above picture – or fixing the pipe to the inside of the frame with screws.

This can then be covered over with polythene or insect mesh to protect your plants, and can be easily moved around the garden according to your needs.

Raised beds should be turned over with a garden fork to freshen them up, and new composting material added to the mix. Do not use topsoil in a Raised Bed garden if at all possible, as this has a tendency to firm-up and defeat the main objective of a Raised Bed Garden – which should be easy to dig and maintain.

Traditional vegetable garden beds should be turned over with a fork before the last of the winter frosts. This frost helps to break up the soil and also to kill destructive pests that have over-wintered in the soil.

If you are fortunate enough to have a pig or two, then let them root around in the ground for a weeks or so before planting. The will happily root out any grubs and slugs hiding in the soil – and fertilize the ground in the process!

Chickens are also quite good for this, as they will scratch around all day looking for insects and grubs.

Straw Bale Gardening

Straw or Hay bales can also be used very successfully for growing vegetables, and in fact this technique has been growing in popularity over recent years.

Again, I have a separate book on the subject that goes into great detail, but the basics are simply this.

Select your Straw or Hay bale or bales, and place them on edge (pointy straw side facing up) in a suitable position where they will not need to be moved later on, as this is virtually impossible.

Prime the bale with water mixed with nitrogen rich fertilizer for a period of 12-15 days. This will cause the bale to begin 'cooking' and allow it to cool down enough for planting to begin.

To plant your veggies simply dig a suitable pot-sized hole in the bale and fill this with a good growing medium before inserting your plant.

Make sure your bales are kept well watered especially over hot dry summers, and you may be pleasantly surprised at the results!

Choose Straw over Hay bales if possible as hay bales can result in a lot of weed growth. (hay bales are made from grass whilst Straw is the by-product of mainly barley, wheat, and oats.)

Straw bales are by their nature carbon based and so have little or zero nutrient value. This means that the nutrients have to be added in the way described.

Hay bales on the other hand are nitrogen rich and so could be the preferred option – if it weren't for the fact they can be completely overcome with wild grass – it's no fun trying to mow a hay bale :)

One of the advantages of this type of gardening is that it allows for slightly earlier planting. This is because the bale heats up and allows the plant to thrive in the warmer temperatures.

If this bale is covered with a cloche or similar polythene covering, then it can be used even earlier – the same way as a Hot Bed – as the plant is protected from the cold air and the mini-polytunnel warms up inside.

Complete instructions along with the pros and cons of straw vs hay bales can be found in my book on the subject.

Compost:

This is also a good time to get the compost heap or heaps sorted out. Choose the best well-rotted compost for your seedlings. This should be reasonably dry and crumbly to the touch.

It should not smell or stink of manure as this would indicate that the decomposition process was not complete. Instead it should have a rich earthy or mushroom-like smell.

Sieve out any large pieces with a garden sieve and mix 50/50 with clean sand to make an ideal potting compost for seeds.

A triple bin composter such as the one below that has been made from old pallets, is ideal for your on-going composting efforts. You can see from this picture that the newest material has been put into the right-hand bin, with the second year in the middle and third year (completed compost) to the far left.

This is not a definite, but rather a general rule of composting – no need to get too precious about it!

The compost material that is not quite ready for use should be turned over with a garden fork to increase air flow, which in turn accelerates the composting process.

With all the groundwork done regarding your planting methods and choices, along with the soil preparation and other tasks, it is time to consider the vegetables themselves.

<u>MY NOTES/THINGS TO DO</u>

MY NOTES/THINGS TO DO

2: Choosing The Plants

Again much of this will have been done over the quieter months of winter, now however it needs a final going-over before the orders are placed.

Vegetables that are liable to thrive in the cooler months of early Spring, and struggle as the weather warms up. It is imperative that you know *when* to plant as well as *what* to plant in order not to be fighting the laws of nature – and fighting a losing battle!

In order to do this properly it is essential you know what Plant Hardiness planting zone you are in. This will tell you what the expected temperatures are likely to be in your region, and what is likely to grow effectively in the early season.

Plant hardiness zone maps for the USA and UK follow, other zone maps can be found online at http://www.edible-landscape-design.com/plant-hardiness-zone.html

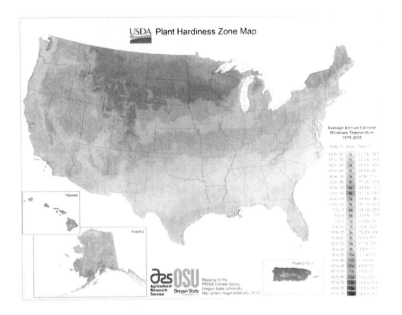

MY NOTES/THINGS TO DO

Average Annual Extreme Minimum Temperature 1976-2005

Temp (F)	Zone	Temp (C)
-60 to -55	1a	-51.1 to -48.3
-55 to -50	1b	-48.3 to -45.6
-50 to -45	2a	-45.6 to -42.8
-45 to -40	2b	-42.8 to -40
-40 to -35	3a	-40 to -37.2
-35 to -30	3b	-37.2 to -34.4
-30 to -25	4a	-34.4 to -31.7
-25 to -20	4b	-31.7 to -28.9 }
-20 to -15	5a	-28.9 to -26.1
-15 to -10	5b	-26.1 to -23.3
-10 to -5	6a	-23.3 to -20.6
-5 to 0	6b	-20.6 to -17.8
0 to 5	7a	-17.8 to -15
5 to 10	7b	-15 to -12.2
10 to 15	8a	-12.2 to -9.4
15 to 20	8b	-9.4 to -6.7
20 to 25	9a	-6.7 to -3.9
25 to 30	9b	-3.9 to -1.1
30 to 35	10a	-1.1 to 1.7
35 to 40	10b	1.7 to 4.4
40 to 45	11a	4.4 to 7.2
45 to 50	11b	7.2 to 10
50 to 55	12a	10 to 12.8
55 to 60	12b	12.8 to 15.6
60 to 65	13a	15.6 to 18.3
65 to 70	13b	18.3 to 21.1

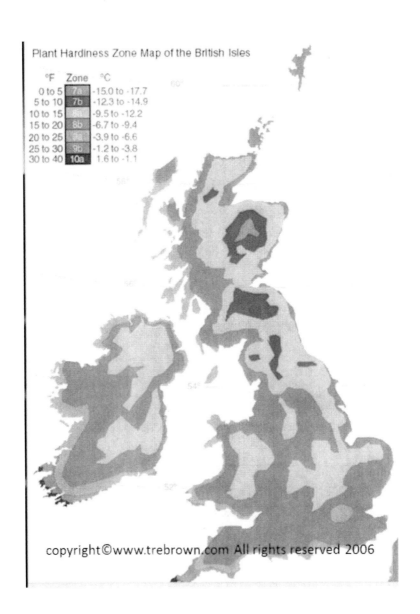

Armed with this information as well as local knowledge, you will have a good idea of what to plant and what to avoid if you are to have a reasonable chance of success.

With that said, there are certain popular choices when it comes to Spring planting. The exact time of planting, and whether to plant seed directly into the ground, or to choose to plant your seedling forced-on, depends largely on where you live and the method(s) that you choose.

The chart on the following page highlights many of the popular hardy and semi-hardy vegetables to begin the season with, as well as the time scales involved before they reach maturity.

The temperatures recorded are the ground temperatures for minimum and optimum growth.

A typical plan for growing vegetables should include elements of Companion planting to increase yield through organic or natural means.

Companion planting methods have been used for many centuries to improve plant yield and care through considerate planting. This means that the nutritional, and other needs of the plant are cared for by growing suitable 'companions' alongside your chosen vegetables.

The following chapter on proper crop rotation rules - extracted from my book **Vegetable Gardening Basics** - should also be followed in order to get the best out of your vegetable plot.

Crop Rotation:

In order for any vegetable patch to prosper and give out the best results, general rules must be observed and perhaps the most important of these are crop rotational rules.

As mentioned briefly in the preceding chapter, crop rotation is essential in 'spreading the love' as well as the risk, when it comes to pest and nutrient control. With that in mind, you will find listed below a selection of do's and don'ts with regard to vegetable categories and their requirements.

Vegetables are ranked into 4 main categories, and they are..

1. **Legumes**: french beans, peas, runner beans, broad beans

2. **Root vegetables**: radish, carrot, potato, onion, garlic, beetroot, swede, sweet potato, shallots, leeks

3. **Leafy greens**: spinach, cabbage, cauliflower, broccoli, lettuce, spinach

4. **Fruit-bearing**: tomato, sweetcorn, cucumber, squash, pumpkin, courgette, strawberry, pepper, aubergine, water melon

You must also bear in mind that plants also belong to 'families.' For instance it is not clear from this list, but tomato and potato are in fact in the same family and so will attract the same pests and use up the same soil nutrients. This of course means that they should be planted separately wherever possible.

As the goal of proper crop management means that you do not wish to deplete the soil nutrients by planting vegetables with the same requirements either together or following one after the other, it is important also to know the families to which they belong.

Brassicas (Cabbage Family):
Brussels sprout, broccoli, all varieties of cabbage, kohl rabi, cauliflower, kale, pak choi, radish, rocket, swede, turnip.

Legumes (Bean & Pea Family):
Mange tout, pea, borlotti, runner, French and broad beans.

Solanaceae (Potato & Tomato Family):
Aubergine, potato, peppers, tomato.

Umbelliferae (carrot & Root Family):
Celery, celeriac, fennel, carrot, coriander, parsnip, parsley, dill.

Alliums (Onion Family):
Garlic, shallot, chive, leek and all varieties of onion.

Cucurbits (Squash & Marrow Family):
Cucumber, courgette, marrow, melon, pumpkin, squash.

Chenopodiaceae (Beetroot Family):
Beetroot, perpetual spinach, Swiss chard, spinach,

Miscellaneous Plants:
All fruit, mint, oregano, rosemary, sage, basil, lettuce, cress, Jerusalem artichoke, sweetcorn, asparagus, okra, salsify, corn salad, chicory

Brassicas follow Legumes:
The general rule in crop rotation is that Brassicas follow Legumes. This means that you would sow crops such as cauliflower, cabbage and kale on soil previously occupied with peas and beans. This is due to the fact that the Brassicas will benefit from the nitrogen rich soil that the Legumes have left behind.

Roots don't like rich soil:
Root vegetables should not be planted in very rich or over fertilized soil, as the leafy part of the veg will bloom at the expense of the edible root itself. Whenever possible, plant parsnips for instance the season after more demanding crops such as brassicas have broken down the rich soil.

3: Seed Propagation

Planting from seed may perhaps be a daunting thought for some, as it can be quite laborious and fraught with potential failure!

However by following the tips in this section, you will find that one of the great advantages is that you can 'steal a march' on the seasons and get a good early start to your veggie garden.

Other reasons for choosing to grow from seed is that it is much cheaper than purchasing young plants from the garden center. Planting from seed also means that you will have a larger choice of plants to choose from, as typically garden centres can only stock a limited choice of the more popular varieties.

To successfully grow from seed you need the proper conditions to ensure good germination and healthy growth, as outlined below.

1: Choose the right containers with at least 2-3 inches depth of growing medium. This can be in the form of seedling trays or bio-degradable pots or any number of types of containers.

2: The growing medium itself must be suitable for the plants growing needs. A mix of 50% compost to 50% sand is suitable for most veggies. Alternatively use a mix of 1/3 vermiculite, 1/3 compost, 1/3 clean sand. Garden soil is not considered ideal in most cases.

With this mix, the vermiculite will act as a water retainer while the sand provides natural drainage, and the compost provides the required nutrients.

3: Protect from cold weather or late frosts by means of a cloche or cold-frame as outlined in earlier chapters.

4: Water adequately, but do not over-do it. The soil should be moist but not wet. Allowing short periods where the top-soil dries out completely will help discourage mould growth on the young seedlings.

5: Careful timing is needed to ensure the young plant will reach maturity as and when you need it to. This will also determine when you should begin propagation so that the young plant has the best chance of survival when planted out.

6: If in doubt, refer to the packet to find the optimum temperature needed for germination to take place. Most vegetables prefer a soil temperature of between 55-65F to stimulate germination.

Air temperature is best kept around 70-75F otherwise the young plants are likely to sprout and grow 'leggy.'

Actual months in which to plant your seeds will vary slightly according to which method you use, as per the previous chapters.

7: Remember to expose your young seedlings to maximum light as soon as they have germinated to avoid them sprouting, as in the previous note.

8: Evening and early morning temperatures can drop dramatically in the early Spring, so cover your young plants with garden fleece or other light material during these times.

A late frost can bring to ruin all your hard work and preparation if you are not vigilant.

If you are using a cold-frame, you can also install a night heater that will keep the cold at bay.

9: As a general rule, minimal disturbance is advised when it comes to transplanting your seedlings to their permanent position in the garden.

10: Roots such as carrots and parsnips should not be transplanted at all, as they are prone to go slightly crazy as the following picture reveals.

Choose instead to sow them in their 'permanent' position, covered over with a hoop cloche or similar. The soil should be totally stone-free, and thinning-out should be done by clipping a 1-2 inch space between the seedlings, rather than pulling out the excess plants.

Simply clip the unwanted seedlings at ground level. This is to minimise disruption to the neighbouring carrots and to help against possible attack by the dreaded carrot fly!

The soil mix of 50% sand to 50% fine compost suits carrots and parsnips ideally as it is obstacle-free and likely to produce fine straight carrots.

4: Plant Protection

There are many things to consider especially early on in the season, when damaging frost and hungry critters compete for your young plants. This chapter will offer tips and advice to protect your plants from both.

Even in the early Spring, destructive pests such as cutworm can cause severe damage to early planted crops such as beans and peas. Fortunately the solutions to these problems are often quite simple.

To protect your beans and peas from the ravages of cutworm or even nibbling mice, try growing them inside a cardboard toilet-roll insert.

Alternatively you can also use 1/34 plastic plumbers pipe cut to 4 inch lengths. These can be used year on year compared to the cardboard inserts which will only last a season – but are equally effective.

Below you will see a picture of some plastic pipes I had to install over my young leek plants as the mice were determined to nibble them away to nothing!

The pipes did the trick though. It's not that they could not gain access to the young plants if they really wanted to – the pipes just make the proposition less attractive to them!

As the warmer weather of early spring progresses then flying pests such as the cabbage moth or butterfly can become a real pest. Before you know it your brassicas are crawling with caterpillars that will demolish your hard work in no time.

The simplest way to deal with these and other pests is to cover your brassicas with either garden fleece or fine nylon netting.

This is simple and 100% effective – providing you do the job properly and allow no areas for the butterflies to gain access :)

Raised beds are particularly easy to cover in this way. However everything from hoop-cloche's to simply throwing fleece over your plants will protect them quite effectively.

A row cloche like the one above is made by simple polythene pipe loops sunk into the ground at each end then covered over with insect mesh or polythene.

Floating row covers are similar to the row cloche above, but instead of being fixed to wires they are simply placed loosely over the plants, leaving enough room for the plant to grow.

This cover is held down at the sides by sinking the material into the ground and covering with soil.

If you are growing in an exposed position, put up wind barriers to stop your plants 'burning' as the wind dehydrates them faster than they can replace the moisture.

A wicker fence can look particularly attractive in a garden area, but any fence or barrier made from hazel or willow for instance will do the job.

Just beware that the fence does not shade the plants too much from the life-giving effects of the natural sunlight.

Bear in mind that a fence does not have to be of solid construction in order to give good wind protection. In fact a simple vertical rail fence like the one below will offer reasonable protection from the wind, and allow sunlight and airflow through to your plants.

You can also use the fence as a climbing frame/support to grow your beans, peas, cucumber or other climbing plants against.

If you are serious about protecting your fruit berries, then a nylon mesh-covered cage or frame does the job beautifully!

5: Making Good Friends!

We all know the benefits to be gained by surrounding ourselves with good companions. Folks who will 'watch our backs' when times get rough, and protect as well as feed and nurture us throughout our lifetimes.

If we have kids, then we worry about the negative impact some other children may have on them; whilst we try and encourage the 'good kids' to hang around.

Ok…this is maybe laying it on a bit thick :) However, it turns out that plants are exactly the same! (ok they maybe can't make the same choices we can – I'll grant you that.)

All joking apart. If you want your veggies to really benefit from their environment, then growing them alongside plants that will help them prosper is a valuable start.

Known as 'Companion Planting.' This is a technique that has been practiced probably since we ceased to become hunter-gatherers and settled down to grow our food.

This is a huge subject, and yes you've guessed it – I have a book specifically aimed at this whole process :) (link above).

However for the sake of this Spring Gardening book I will include possibly the most important aspect for this season.

That is, what to plant alongside young plants in order to get the best out of them in the coming summer season.

Check out the Companion Planting chart on the next page (which you will also find in the Winter Gardening issue). Here you will find a selection of plants and their good/bad companions.

MY NOTES/THINGS TO DO

VEGGIES	GOOD COMPANION	BAD COMPANION
Asparagus	Tomato, Parsley, Basil	
Beans	Beetroot, cabbage, celery, carrot, cucumber, corn, squash, pea's, potatoes, radish, strawberry.	garlic, shallot or onions
Beets	broccoli, brussels sprouts, bush beans, cabbage, cauliflower	charlock, field mustard, pole beans
Cabbage	cucumber, lettuce, potato, onion, spinach, celery.	strawberries
Carrots	beans, peas, onions, lettuce, tomato, leeks, and radish	Dill
Celery	Bean, tomato and cabbage family	Corn, Irish potato and aster flowers
Corn	Potato, pumpkin, squash, tomato, cucumber	tomatoes
Cucumber	cabbage, beans, cucumber, radish, tomato	late potatoes
Eggplant	beans, peas, spinach, tarragon, thyme	
Garlic	cabbage, cane fruits, fruit trees, tomatoes	peas, beans
Lettuce	Cabbage, carrot, beet, onion, and strawberry	cabbage family
Melon	pumpkin, radish, corn, and squash	
Onions	cabbage family, beet, tomato, pepper, strawberry, peas, and chard	beans, peas
Parsley	asparagus, carrot, tomato and corn	mint
Peas	beans, carrot, corn and radish	garlic leeks, onions, shallots
Peppers	Tomato, eggplant, carrot and onion	fennel, kohlrabi
Potatoes	bean, cabbage, squash and peas	apples, cherries, cucumbers, pumpkins, sunflowers, tomatoes
Pumpkin	Melon eggplant and corn	Potato, raspberry
Radish	carrot, cucumber, bean, pea, melon	hyssop
Squash	melon, pumpkin, tomato, beans, cucumber, onion	Potato, tomato
Strawberry	bean, lettuce, onion and spinach	Cabbage, broccoli, Brussels sprouts
Tomatoes	celery, cucumber, asparagus, parsley, pepper and carrot	fennel, kohlrabi, potatoes

Following the information in the chart above will ensure that your veggies have the best chance of success – considering all other requirements have been met of course!

Quite apart from using cloches or polytunnels to protect your young seedling, you can also use upturned plant pots or even cardboard boxes for individual plants.

Another subject to be covered now, is the fairly obvious but non-the-less important issue of Plant Support for climbers and free-standing but weak-stalked vegetables.

MY NOTES/THINGS TO DO

6: Plant Support

As you may imagine, there are numerous ways to support your vegetables – but why exactly do they need support?

There are a number of good reasons why <u>some</u> plants need support, here are just 3 of them..

1: To prevent fruit-laden branches from trailing on the ground, thus making the fruits vulnerable to insect or animal attack.

2: If fruits such as tomatoes are not supported then the main – or fruit-bearing - stem will collapse, resulting in damage to the plant and loss of the fruits.

3: Supported plants are also able to get the best benefit from the sunshine as well as air-flow (helps prevent mould) and pollinating insects.

With that said, Spring is the perfect time to either make repairs to your existing plant supports or indeed to make up new ones for the coming season.

Some examples of supports for fruit and vegetable plants can be seen in the pictures/diagrams below. But there are numerous ways to support your plants and indeed many different materials that can be used to good effect.

Fences, canes, poles and posts can all be used in conjunction with fencing wire, nylon netting or garden twine to effect some version of these examples.

Any garden wall can be used most effectively to run wires and support Espaliered fruit trees such as the pears in the examples above.

Peas and beans are easily supported using canes and/or nylon netting. In the picture above you will see the cardboard inserts from toilet rolls to protect against cutworm and nibbling mice.

Vegetables grown in straw bales can be easily supported and protected using a pole at each end and wires strung between to support beans, peas, cucumber, tomato or any number of veggies.

Beans are strong climbers and will happily grow up canes set at 5-6 feet high.

Below is a classic arrangement for supporting raspberries and other climbing fruit bearers. The horizontal lines can be from 2 to 3 strings each side typically.

In most cases the wires or supporting strings are set at around 9 inches apart. The supporting posts must be anchored well enough to take the strain of the wires as they are tensioned and also the weight of the plant as the fruit begins to develop.

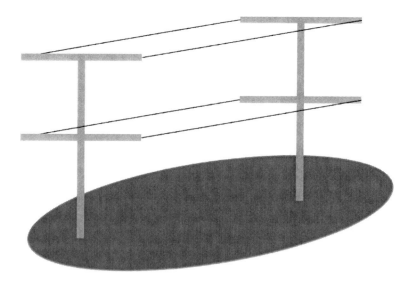

In older established situations, the frame-work should be thoroughly inspected and treated before the season begins to kill any over-wintering pests that may have taken up residence.

Likewise old supporting canes should be inspected before use to be sure there are no pests lurking inside the hollow tubes.

7: Odds & Ends!

Finally, as all gardeners are too aware, there is always more to be done around the productive garden.

Here is a short list of everything else I could think of that needs tended to during the spring/summer months – there is no doubt more!

1: Clean the greenhouse glass whilst access is easy. Clean away any whitener you have used to shade the plants during the hot summer of last year, and remove any old vines etc that are blocking the light.

Clear out any spiders and other critters with a stiff brush, then spray the area with a mixture of peppermint oil and water to keep them away. 15-20 drops peppermint oil to a hand sprayer filled with water will suffice.

Do the same with cold-frames that you may be using.

2: Dig out and check your greenhouse heaters and any other electrical equipment you may be using, to be sure they are fully operational and there is not any broken leads or exposed wiring.

I once almost killed myself when I used an electric drill which I had not noticed had a split in the cable – a truly shocking experience that would have never happened if I had properly checked it beforehand.

It would also have never happened if I had used an RCD (Residual Current Device) to trip the power supply! Hmmm

3: Clear away any drainage ditches and guttering that may have become clogged with falling debris over the winter. Put the old organic material straight into the compost pile.

4: Fence and trellis repairs are also best done at this time, before the weeds and foliage have time to grow and make access difficult.

5: If you have bare ground that you are not intending using for a few weeks or months, cover it over with black plastic or weed fabric.

This will make it so much easier to manage when the time comes to start planting it out - and save you having to weed it .

6: If your soil has a ph level below 6.2, then it will benefit from the addition of lime to balance it out. Add Dolomite lime (the finest grind) 3-4 weeks before planting out, then cover over with plastic to prevent runoff.

7: Now is also the time to give the lawn a good raking out to remove any rubbish that has gathered, and to allow air and sunlight to the new growth.

Bare spots can be repaired by adding some grass seed to a bucked of topsoil or potting mix, then scattering over the bald patch.

8: Apply Horticultural oil spray to fruit trees and shrubs just as the buds begin to swell. Do this ten days or so later to control pear leaf blister mite and pear psylla. Apply oil spray to pears just as the buds begin to swell and then again 10 days later to control pear psylla and pear leaf blister mite.

Apply this Dormant oil to fruit trees or shrubs that have a history of aphid, spider mite or scale infestations.

9: Early Spring is generally the last chance to prune the fruit trees before they begin to blossom. Later than this can result in stress to the plant and a subsequent loss of fruit.

10: Growing Asparagus? This is one of the earliest crops in the 'traditional' vegetable garden. The early spring is the time to clear away any old dead material, and fertilize to encourage the new growth as soon as the shoots appear.

A balanced fertilizer containing equal amounts of nitrogen, phosphorus and potassium, is ideal for Asparagus.

11: Finally, check all your hand tools. Sharpen the blades and oil the working parts. If you didn't have the lawnmower serviced before you put it away, do it now – before you need it to work!

Spring may well be here already by the time you read this book – which means that summer is just around the corner!

<u>MY NOTES/THINGS TO DO</u>

MY NOTES/THINGS TO DO

Episode 4: Gardening Tips For Summer

THE VEGETABLE GARDENERS TOP JOBS FOR THE SUMMER GROWING SEASON.

BY

JAMES PARIS

Published By

www.deanburnpublications.com

Blog: http://www.planterspost.com

Introduction:

If Spring is the season of hope for the vegetable gardener, then Summer is definitely the season of anticipation! Arguably most of the hard preparatory work has been accomplished. The fruit & vegetables have been planted and are now thriving in your well-tended vegetable beds, and you are eagerly anticipating enjoying the fruits of your labour – if not already doing so.

Crops such as early potatoes, asparagus, mushrooms, lettuce, radish and other salads are usually the first on the plate. While over-wintered crops such as, beets, parsnips, carrots, garlic and some brassicas for example, may have been enjoyed in the late spring.

This is especially the case for those who live in the hotter climates of Florida, the gulf coast and Texas for instance where a spring harvest from a fall planting is the normal practice.

For those in more temperate or cooler northern climates however, most of the mid to late summer in my mind is spent on three main things. Plant & Plot maintenance (feed, support, and protection). Harvesting, and planning for the fall season.

There are of course other jobs around the veggie plot to keep yourself busy – but these three in particular encompass the main tasks for the summer growing season.

With that in mind, this episode of 'Gardening Seasons' will concentrate on these areas in particular and other aspects of vegetable gardening in general.

MY NOTES/THINGS TO DO

Plant & Plot Maintenance

Caring for your plants covers a wide range of tasks that need attended to in order to get the best out of them. From general plant maintenance, to pest control, feeding and protection from pests; keeping your vegetables in top form is essential.

CATERPILLAR NIGHTMARE!

How do you deal with caterpillars, and what happens when the carrots are threatened with carrot fly and the cabbage leaves are turning yellow? Heavy cropping plants in particular will need some support, to avoid damage to both plants and fruit. These and other issues are discussed in this chapter.

Support:

Make sure even before you plant out your fruit or vegetable plants, that you have allowed for suitable support. This is especially the case with heavy fruit-bearing crops such as tomatoes or cucumber for example.

For bush tomato plants a wire cage is ideal. This can be constructed by simply cutting a section of weld-mesh about 3 foot long, then pulling in both ends to form a tube effect.

Place this mesh tube over the tomato plants to give them support. This is also an ideal support for cucumber, courgette, squash etc.

For vine or cordon tomato plants, a simple support made from a cane or even string loosely tied to the base of the plant and secured overhead, is usually sufficient.

Horizontal wires strung between two posts will also suffice as in the picture below. The growing vine can then be secured to the horizontal wires.

Climbers such as peas and beans can be trained to climb virtually anything that will offer to support them. While beans climb by winding themselves around the vertical supports such as poles or canes sunk into the ground; peas send out tendrils to cling to anything within reach.

Protection:

As the summer season progresses, your fruit and vegetables will need protection from a number of directions. The weather, destructive insects, disease and pests.

The weather of course depends on where you live. Arizona has different weather related problems than Florida for example!

Storm or wind damage – which can dehydrate your plants - can be prevented by making sure your plants have an adequate wind-break. This can be a simple fence of wood slats, or a more solid construction such as a beech hedge or even concrete wall.

Anything that will break the prevailing wind and offer protection to your plants by preventing them drying out or being damaged.

Protection from birds is especially relevant for fruit-bearing bushes such as raspberries, blackberries, blackcurrants etc. In the case of many vegetables such as brassicas however, birds can be your best friend as they pluck away caterpillars and other destructive bugs.

Make sure there-fore that before your fruit trees or strawberries begin to bear fruit, you have adequate protection in place. This is best done with nylon bird-netting placed over a cage or frame-work of some sort.

Protection from insects is an on-going task throughout the growing season, but mid-summer is a time when the battle tends to be in full swing!

Brassicas in particular can suffer badly from caterpillar infestation, mainly thanks to the cabbage butterfly or cabbage moth.

These sweet innocent-looking white butterflies flit around the cabbage patch and lay clusters of yellow eggs under the leaves of the cabbages. These hatch out within a few days to form hungry caterpillars that will cause utter devastation to your precious veggies!

The best and most effective way to deal with this problem is to cover your brassicas with butterfly mesh or netting. Make sure that you have adequate space between the netting and the leaves, otherwise the cabbage moth will still manage to lay her eggs!

Raised beds are particularly easy to do this with by forming a simple loop system with some plumbers pipe and covering with netting. Otherwise stick some canes around the garden. Top them off with a small plant-pot, then throw the netting over them.

This will keep the netting well away from your plants and offer maximum protection for the least effort.

Gardeners fleece also offers excellent protection against a number of destructive pests as well as against inclement weather, offering shade and helping to retain moisture in the ground.

Fleece can be used to protect your carrots from the carrot fly, and at the same time offer wind protection.

Natural insecticidal sprays can also be used very effectively against aphids and other soft-bodied insects.

A good all-rounder is easily made by adding a garlic clove and a squirt of washing up liquid into a hand sprayer filled with water. Leave for a few days to infuse then spray directly onto the plant.

This will also help against powdery mildew.

Alternatively add 2-3 tablespoons of white vinegar to 1 pint of water in a hand sprayer and spray directly onto the insects. Test this first on a small area of plant though as some plants will not react well to the acid in the vinegar.

You can test the effectiveness against the insects by increasing the vinegar dose – but keep a close watch on your plants.

Chilli pepper spray is also very effective against a number of insects. Boil up 2-3 hot peppers in a pint of water for 15 minutes or so. Let the mixture cool down before adding to your hand sprayer and applying directly to the insects.

Slugs: Slugs are often regarded as public enemy no 1 – and with good cause. 1 big fat slug can devastate young seedlings overnight, so adequate care must taken to avoid or at least reduce the damage from these critters.

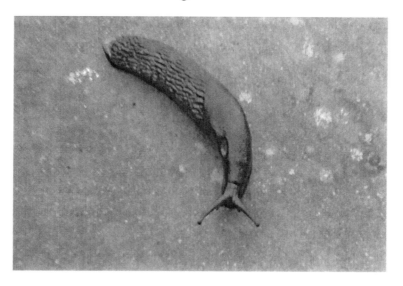

Fortunately there are a number of tried-and-tested ways to deal with slugs.

Physical removal: Yes this is a bit yucky, however it is very effective. Go out a night after dark with a torch when they are most active, and simply pluck them away from your plants and into a container for disposal.

Beer traps can be set by adding some beer to a small jar and sinking it into the ground near your plants. The slugs are lured by the yeasty smell of the beer and drown in the traps.

Chemical Slug pellets are generally not a good idea – though they are extremely effective! Why are they not a good idea? Simply because they tend to kill a lot more than the slugs you are targeting.

Hedgehogs (the gardeners best friend), toads, frogs and birds will all die if they eat a pellet-contaminated slug.

However all is not lost – there are now organic 'friendly' slug pellets available on the market shelves.

Broken egg shells and copper pipe are things that slugs do not like to cross over, whilst sheep-wool pellets can also be extremely effective in this regard.

Slug nematodes can also be purchased and are an extremely effective and environmentally friendly option – though they can be a little expensive.

MY NOTES/THINGS TO DO

MY NOTES/THINGS TO DO

Pruning & Trimming:

Although it's fair to say that most pruning work is done in the early spring or late autumn period; summer is a time when general pruning, layering and clipping for maintenance purposes is necessary.

This is particularly the case for fruit trees/shrubs. Tomato plants need constant attention to cut or nip away any side shoots (vine varieties only).

After the plant has grown to between 4 and 7 trusses it is time to stop upward growth by nipping away the top shoot. Remove the leaves to about halfway up the main stem to encourage fruit growth and discourage disease.

Peas and beans should be harvested regularly in order to encourage continued growth. With runner beans in particular, do not let them grow beyond 5-6 inches or they will get tough and fibrous.

Layering: This is also the time to consider layering your berry bushes to encourage new growth for the following year. This is done by simply pulling down one of the branches and pinning it to the ground.

This will encourage the branch to set roots and grow of its own accord. This new growth can then be detached and planted to create a new berry bush.

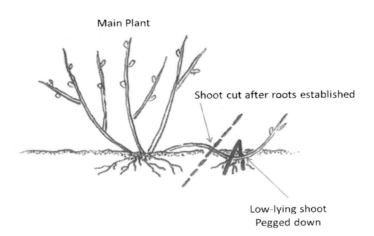

Berries can also be 'mounded up' to produce shoots that are suitable for transplanting as they establish their own root system.

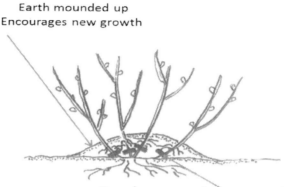

Regularly check over your fruit and berry trees and cut away any dead, damaged or diseased branches. Fruit in general grows to the outside of the plants so it is beneficial to keep the inside areas trimmed and clutter free.

This encourages fruit growth and improves air flow to the center of the plant, which in turn reduces the risk of disease through bad ventilation.

Fruit trees such as apples and pears should be pruned in the late summer to encourage crops for the following year, and to allow light into the middle of the tree.

New shoots (laterals) should be cut back to with 3 buds of the main stem after they have reached a length of approximately 8 inches or more.

New shoots growing from existing side shoots (sub-laterals) should be cut back to one leaf above the basal cluster. Vigorous vertical growth should be cut back completely.

Strawberries that have been rooted from runners should be cut and transplanted at this time, to be sure of strong fruit-bearing growth in the following year. Plant 9-12 inches apart.

Squash & Courgettes: To encourage branching and more fruits, nip away the growing tips of squash and courgettes. Aubergines should have the growing tip nipped off once they have produced 5-6 fruits.

Cucumbers as best trained to grow upwards rather than trailing on the ground. Tie their long stems to wires or frame supports.

Feeding:

The early to late summer season is also a time when many fruits and vegetables are demanding extra feed in order to facilitate the growth of fruits.

During this time a weekly feed of nitrogen/potassium is recommended to encourage abundant cropping. There are 2 main ways to achieve this. The first is to simply go out and buy chemical fertilizer from the store.

The second is to produce your own easy-to-make organic fertilizer. This is free in most cases, and very simple to do. Ok, there is a third way – buy organic fertilizer!

Organic fertilizers or 'tea' can be produced from several sources, but is mostly made the same way for all. For this example I will use the most popular tea of all – comfrey tea. Full of potassium and nitrogen it has all the minerals needed for most fruit and vegetable plants.

1: Take a large clump of comfrey and add to a pail of water. Weigh it down with a heavy stone so that it is completely submerged.

There should be enough comfrey to take up approximately one third of the garden pail or bucket.

2: Let soak for 10 days to mature and infuse properly.

3: Mix it with water at a 15 to 1 ratio (15 parts water), before feeding your plants with the mix.

This can be 'topped up' throughout the season. Don't worry when you see black, brackish, smelly water – the plants love it!

In fact just about anything organic will break down in water and produce minerals to feed your plants. And especially in the case of weed-tea, its mostly completely free!

Other materials that can be used to make great tea include stinging nettles, compost, chicken manure, horse manure, sheep manure (leave manures for at least 4 weeks before use), seaweed and general garden weeds.

When using animal manure, only use manure from herbivores to prevent the spread of disease-causing bacteria and pathogens such as E Coli, that may be present in carnivore or omnivore manure.

Always use protective gloves and take all necessary hygiene precautions when handling manure.

Harvesting:

Harvesting your crops is of course something that happens throughout the growing season. Winter crops that have been planted in the previous Autumn such as cabbage, turnip, broccoli and carrots for instance; have already been harvested and eaten.

1st and 2nd Early potatoes will have been harvested by this time along with early onions perhaps.

Legumes such as peas and beans are harvested throughout the season. As are tomato plants, cucumber, squash.

Harvesting your crops is an ideal time to inspect your veggies for things such as insect infestation, disease or general ill health of your plants.

Take care when pulling away the fruits no matter if they are beans or tomatoes or whatever. Torn, badly handled fruit stems are only going to be detrimental to your plants in the long term, and will only encourage disease or insect damage.

Late onions are best left on the ground surface for a few days after harvesting. This will dry them naturally and toughen the skins for storage in a cool dry place.

Apples are harvested by a simple twist and pull. If the apple does not come away then it is not ready to pluck. They are best stored away from other fruits and vegetables as they produce ethylene gas.

This gas encourages the ripening or growth of vegetables in particular. Do not store apples next to potatoes for example, as the potatoes are likely to sprout as a result.

Main crop potatoes should be ready to harvest by late summer. This is indicated by the plant drying up and dying after it has flowered fully.

This technique has the added benefit of no weeding!

Courgettes and pumpkins also grow well with this method as the fabric not only controls weeds, but warms the surrounding area.

Throughout the growing period however, be sure to mound-up your potatoes with soil to prevent exposure to the sunlight. Failure to do this will result in the exposed tubers going green and poisonous – do **NOT** eat these green potatoes!

Alternatively you can grow them under weed fabric as in the picture above.

<u>MY NOTES/THINGS TO DO</u>

Winter Planting

It may seem a little strange, talking about winter planting at this time! However late Summer/Autumn is the time for planning and planting out your garden with next year's harvest in mind.

Indeed cool season vegetables such as winter cabbage, cauliflower, swedes, and brussels sprouts can be planted at this time for consumption throughout the winter period.

Winter cabbage varieties such as Huron, OS Cross and Danish Ball Head are especially good for late season growing.

Parsnips take about 110 days to mature, so time your harvest to be ready after the first winter frosts. However plant whilst the soil temperature is still warm enough to encourage propagation.

Parsnips taste much sweeter and tender after being subjected to frost.

Fast-growing carrot varieties such as *Adelaide* can be planted as late as July for a tasty autumn/winter vegetable. Planting as late as November is possible in a greenhouse or polytunnel – something to consider for many late salad vegetable crops.

<u>MY NOTES/THINGS TO DO</u>

Misc Summer Tasks

There are a number of on-going tasks especially suited to the different seasons. However there are also many tasks that need seen to throughout the year in general.

Here are some jobs to get to grips with over the summer period.

1: Compost – See to it that the compost heap is turned over at least every few weeks or so. This will add air to the mix and ensure that the composting process is not stalled due to a lack of oxygen into the mix.

2: Mulching – use your grass cuttings to mulch between your vegetables. This will warm the soil, act as an effective weed suppressant, and feed the soil – as well as encourage the gardeners best friend – worms!

3: Feed – Top up your 'tea's' regularly to ensure a good supply.

4: Water/irrigation – Check your water supply. Rainwater is always better for vegetables so be sure to trap as much of this precious commodity as possible with water butts and barrels.

Be sure to water your plants daily as the demand for water will increase as the weather warms and the fruits start expanding.

Plant pots sunk into the ground around your vegetables will help direct water to the roots of the plants, without undermining the stem base and encouraging rot.

5: Weeding – possibly the least favourite task for the gardener! This can however be alleviated with the proper use of mulches and garden weed fabric, to make life that bit easier.

6: Thinning seedlings – This should not be neglected especially with vegetables, whose growth will be stunted if there is too much competition.

Seedlings such as carrots and parsnips should be thinned with scissors rather than pulled, to prevent root disturbance. In fact most young seedlings are best thinned this way – if you can stand the loss!

7: Repair & Maintenance – Summer is a good time for keeping your veggie plot and accompanying supports, polytunnels, greenhouses, cloches etc in good order.

8: In a hot dry summer period raise the blade settings for the lawnmower, and reduce the amount of cuts. If the grass is cut to short it is likely to wither and die away.

9: Herbs - Pick, dry and freeze your herbs for later use.

10: Clear away any diseased or spent foliage on or around your veggies to keep them healthy and productive.

Authors Notes/Thanks

Finally I would lie to say **A HUGE THANKS** for purchasing this book – it is very much appreciated.

As this is a compilation of the 4 seasons Episodes, I'm sure you will understand that there will be some duplication of material involved throughout this work. This is an inevitable consequence of combining the 4 Episodes in one volume.

Also if you would like further reading on many aspects of gardening in general, then please check out the links below or log into my Amazon author page.

Other Relevant Books By James Paris

Books in This series:
'Seasonal Gardening Jobs'

Episode 1: Gardening Tips For Autumn
Episode 2: Gardening Tips For Winter
Episode 3: Gardening Tips For Spring
Episode 4: Garden Tips For Summer

Other Relevant Books By James Paris

Raised Bed Gardening 5 Book Bundle
Companion Planting
Growing Berries
Square Foot Gardening
Compost 101
Vegetable Gardening Basics
Small Garden Ideas
Straw Bale Gardening
Hot Bed Gardening

James Paris is an **Amazon Best Selling Author**, you can see the full range of books on his Amazon author page at..
http://amazon.com/author/jamesparis

MY NOTES/THINGS TO DO

MY NOTES/THINGS TO DO

MY NOTES/THINGS TO DO

MY NOTES/THINGS TO DO

MY NOTES/THINGS TO DO

CPSIA information can be obtained
at www.ICGtesting.com
Printed in the USA
LVOW08s2319210317
528032LV00008B/159/P